KU-083-427

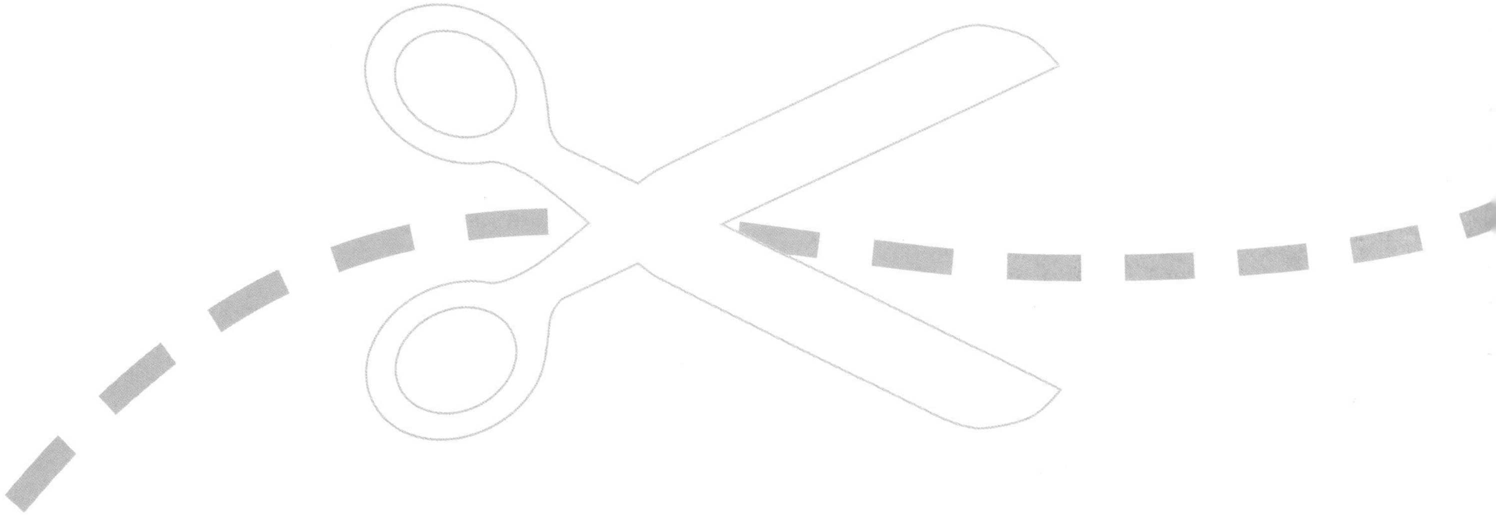

Paper *Cut It*

MARION ELLIOT

David and Charles

A DAVID & CHARLES BOOK

David & Charles is an F+W Publications Inc. company
4700 East Galbraith Road, Cincinnati, OH 45236

First published in 2008

A catalogue record for this book is available from the British Library.

ISBN-13: 978-0-7153-2588-9 hardback
ISBN-10: 0-7153-2588-4 hardback
ISBN-13: 978-0-7153-2587-2 paperback
ISBN-10: 0-7153-2587-6 paperback

Printed in China by SNP Leefung Pte Ltd
for David & Charles
Brunel House Newton Abbot Devon

Executive Editor Cheryl Brown
Desk Editor Bethany Dymond
Head of Design Prudence Rogers
Designer Alistair Barnes
Project Editor Betsy Hosegood
Production Controller Ros Napper
Photographers Karl Adamson and Kim Sayer

Visit our website at www.davidandcharles.co.uk

David & Charles books are available from all good bookshops;
alternatively you can contact our Orderline on 0870 9908222 or write to us at
FREEPOST EX2 110, D&C Direct, Newton Abbot, TQ12 4ZZ (no stamp required UK only);
US customers call 800-289-0963 and Canadian customers call 800-840-5220.

Contents

Introduction

Paper cutting is one of the simplest and most effective of all the paper crafts. You don't need any particular skills to make wonderful paper cuts (apart from the ability to trace a pattern and use a pair of scissors) and yet the results are so satisfying. One of the aspects I most enjoy about the craft is the element of surprise; I am never quite sure how a paper cut is going to look until I unfold the paper for the first time. It can still seem like magic to me.

If you have never attempted paper cutting before, this book will guide you through the various basic techniques you need to make your own stunning creations. Each of the six chapters deals with a simple but exciting paper-cutting skill: single-fold cuts, making garlands, paper lace, unfolded cuts, cut-and-fold sculpture and feathering.

Within each chapter you'll find a range of projects to fire your imagination, starting with a simple card design to demonstrate the technique. Make the cards to try out the techniques first, and create a wonderful stash of greetings cards at the same time. The other projects will take a little longer than the cards, but you should be able to complete any of them in a weekend, and some can be finished in just a matter of a few hours.

As with all paper crafts, paper cutting is absorbing, satisfying and above all, fun. I hope my projects will convey this enjoyment to you and help give you the confidence to embark on your own designs once you've sampled a few of mine.

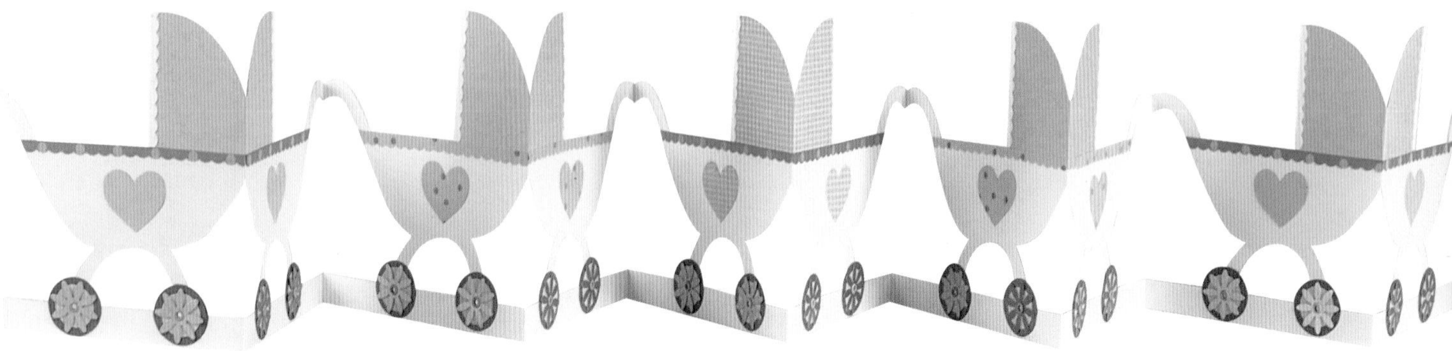

Basic Tool Kit

There are literally thousands of wonderful paper-craft tools to be had, and like most keen hobbyists you'll soon find yourself amassing quite a collection. Once you've got the basics you can start to acquire various cutters, stamps and the like to add decoration or to speed up the making process but to start off with you only need a few basic items, many of which you may already have, especially if you have tried card making or scrapbooking before.

Tracing paper, a **pencil** and **eraser** are needed for tracing and transferring templates. An HB pencil is ideal – softer pencils smudge and create a wide line, while harder pencils can indent the paper.

Lightweight white card is ideal for making templates (see page 8).

A **sharp craft knife** should enable you to cut with complete precision, with ease and comfort of use. Probably the most widely used knives are the scalpel type. For general, everyday work, I use a standard, all-purpose, number 3 handle, with a 10A blade. This handle is fairly slim and is easy to grip. The blades become blunted quite quickly, so change them regularly, as blunt blades will snag your paper. Some knives have retractable blades or plastic safety caps. If yours doesn't, embed the blade in a cork when not in use to prevent accidents.

A **rotating craft knife** is useful for cutting complex designs. This has a small, detachable blade that swivels 360° to allow for extra precision around intricate curves. It takes a bit of getting used to but it does cut very smoothly and accurately.

An **eyelet punch** and **setter** enable you to utilize the ever-expanding range of metal eyelets. I also use the punch to pierce paper in a decorative way – see the Easter Chicken Basket on page 78, for example.

The best **scissors** are the ones you find comfortable to use. My favourite type is the simple paper craft variety with small handles and short, pointed blades. These are easy to handle, make smooth cuts, keep their sharpness for longer and can pierce holes in paper, which is useful if you are cutting out a fiddly design. For best results, keep your scissors solely for cutting paper, and don't cut anything else with them, not even card. This way they will keep their precision, sharpness and accuracy for years.

A **single hole paper punch** is ideal for cutting small, perfect dots, for making holes in tags or for creating decorative borders.

A **metal ruler** should always be used when cutting straight lines with a craft knife. Look out for the safety versions, which have a central channel where you can place your fingers while you cut, to keep them out of the way of the razor-sharp knife blades.

Hint **If you do a lot of card making, a paper cutter is a useful addition to your tool kit. Cutters come in several sizes and are usually marked with measurements to make accurate cutting easier.**

Hint Paper punches are a great for speeding up the cutting process, and I use them for cutting multiples of everyday shapes like hearts and flowers. They are also handy for cutting small, fiddly shapes like snowflakes, effortlessly.

A **cutting mat** is an essential piece of equipment when using a craft knife. The surface of the mat re-seals itself after you have cut into it, so you always have a perfectly smooth surface to work on. You'll also find some useful measuring gauges marked on the mat, which help with accuracy of measuring when cutting long strips of paper, for example. Cutting mats also hold the blade of your craft knife slightly, so it doesn't skid as it would on a polished surface. The mats aren't cheap, but they do protect your work surface, and they come in a useful range of sizes from approximately A5 to A1.

I use **glue stick** for gluing paper to paper because it is pleasant to use and can be spread in a thin, accurate layer. It has a fairly strong bond, but dries slowly enough to allow for re-positioning if necessary. It is important to replace the lid as you work, or the glue will dry out and become useless.

Spray glue is essential for gluing fragile paper and paper-cuts because there is no need to touch the paper or drag glue over it. Hold the can at least 20cm (8in) away and spray lightly, taking several sweeps of spray as required.

PVA glue is a white, all-purpose water-based glue that dries clear. It has a strong bond and is very useful in small amounts for attaching embellishments like sequins to paper and card. However, it can be too liquid to use for sticking layers of paper to each other, as it will soak into the paper and distort the surface. Use an old or inexpensive artist's brush to apply the glue neatly and clean the brush after use.

Clear sticky tape is useful for securing coiled paper or to give added strength to glued joins.

Sticky putty such as Blu Tack is very handy for holding layers of paper together temporarily while you make multiple paper cuts. It is also useful for keeping templates and large-scale tracings in place while you transfer a pattern or image onto your paper.

A **bone folder** is a long, flat tool, a bit like a palette knife. Use it to flatten the crease in folded paper to make it really crisp. It has completely smooth sides, and can be pushed along the fold without snagging or marking the paper.

One-fold Wonders

One-fold cuts are used to produce perfectly symmetrical shapes. You'll need a template of half the design, which you place on folded paper or card, trace and then cut out. No matter how often you use this technique it's always exciting to reveal the completed cutout for the first time.

Traditionally, one-fold paper cutting appears in the folk-art traditions of many countries and it was a favourite for creating beautiful Valentine cards, which could be simple yet elegant or impossibly intricate. That's the joy of this technique – it can be as challenging as you like – but to start with, try something fairly easy such as the delightful Pop-up Butterfly card opposite.

TOOLS AND TECHNIQUES

Perfect paper
Any weight of paper, from tissue paper up to medium-weight (120–150gsm) paper can be successfully folded and cut. Above this weight, the paper becomes difficult to fold neatly, or squarely, and unsightly creases may appear. It's important to be able to fold the paper absolutely flat before placing the template on top. If the fold is slightly raised, the template will not sit square and the resulting shape will not be completely symmetrical.

Folding the paper properly
For best results, fold your paper then place it on a smooth, flat surface. Push the side of a bone folder down the crease to flatten it and make it as sharp as possible.

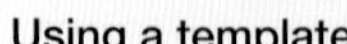

Using a template
When using relatively simple designs it is more accurate to make a template from thin card than to trace the design, particularly if you want to cut a shape more than once. Cut out templates with long, smooth scissor cuts or the edge may become jagged and imperfections will be transferred to every shape that you cut out.

Transferring the design
Place your template on the folded paper right up to the folded edge so that it is on the fold but not overlapping it. Lightly draw around the outside with a hard pencil (HB or above). This will produce a thin, faint line that is much more accurate than the thick line produced by a softer pencil. Make sure that the pencil follows the outline of the template as closely as possible, angling it as necessary.

Pop-up Butterfly Card

Learn the basics of the one-fold technique while making this super three-dimensional butterfly card. You'll find out how to cut on the fold and how to make secondary cuts for added movement and dimension using lightweight card or something flimsier, such as handmade paper. Adding sequins, jewels and beads to the butterfly enables you to transform what is a very simple cut into something truly sophisticated.

you will need

- A4 sheet of lightweight purple card
- A4 sheet of medium-weight green card
- Beading wire
- Clear seed beads
- 2 round silver beads
- Assorted sequins
- Small and large glass stones
- Two 18cm (7in) lengths of 1cm (⅜in) wide raspberry red satin ribbon
- Flat-nosed craft pliers
- Sticky tape
- Basic tool kit

Hint Use your scalpel blade carefully as a tool to help position the sequins exactly where you want them.

1 Fold the purple card in half and press with a bone folder. Trace and transfer the butterfly pattern from page 104 onto thin card and cut it out to make a template. Place it on the purple card, lining up the centre of the template with the fold in the card. Draw around it and cut out the butterfly neatly.

2 Cut along the inner lines of the wings using a craft knife on a cutting mat then fold the inner sections upwards. To make the antennae, cut a 15cm (6in) length of beading wire. Fold it in half, and twist together, leaving about 4cm (1½in) free. Thread seed beads onto the wires, with a silver bead at the top. Twist the ends.

3 Position the antennae on the back of the butterfly, resting the unbeaded end in the fold, as shown. Tape the wire securely in place with clear sticky tape.

4 Turn the butterfly over and decorate it with sequins and glass stones. Cut an 18 x 14cm (7 x 5½in) piece of green card and fold it in half to measure 9 x 14cm (3½ x 5½in). Glue the butterfly to the card, lining up the centre of the butterfly with the fold in the card. Glue a length of ribbon to the top and bottom of the card to finish.

Heart Frame

This first project demonstrates how effective a simple one-fold shape such as a heart can be, especially when it is repeated, here in a magpie collection of complementary paper scraps. The frame itself is made entirely from cardboard. You'll want fairly thin but rigid cardboard like the backing board on a pad of paper because some packaging cardboard is too soft and won't hold its shape. The cardboard is painted afterwards, so it doesn't matter what colour it is. Emulsion paint is ideal for this, and if you use a dry brush with only a little paint on it for each application, you can drag the brush over the cardboard to create a lovely Scandinavian-style drybrush background.

The paper for the hearts has a pretty, faded appearance, inspired by delicate Scandinavian colour schemes, but you could use any range of colours that suits your room scheme or preference.

The overlapping hearts on the frame create a lovely three-dimensional texture. This can be enhanced by using papers of different textures – thick handmade papers, medium-weight paper, coloured tracing paper, vellum and so on.

This delightful frame is ideal for a wedding photograph or any other picture close to your heart, and it can be made to any size required – or even in a different shape.

Heart Frame

you will need

- Dinner plate and saucer to use as templates
- Sheet of thick cardboard larger than your plate
- Sheets and scraps of coordinating handmade and decorative paper
- Thin cord to hang the frame
- Fine sandpaper
- Cream emulsion paint
- Dry artist's flat paintbrush or small decorator's brush
- 2 split pins to attach the hanging cord
- Clear sticky tape or masking tape
- Basic tool kit

Inspiration

This idea converts easily to card making. Simply arrange a ring of hearts on a square card and send it for Valentine's Day, for get-well wishes or even for that special someone's birthday.

Hint **Save time – instead of making the frame yourself simply buy a plain frame or dig out an old one, spruce it up with a coat of paint if needed, and then cut out and stick on the paper hearts.**

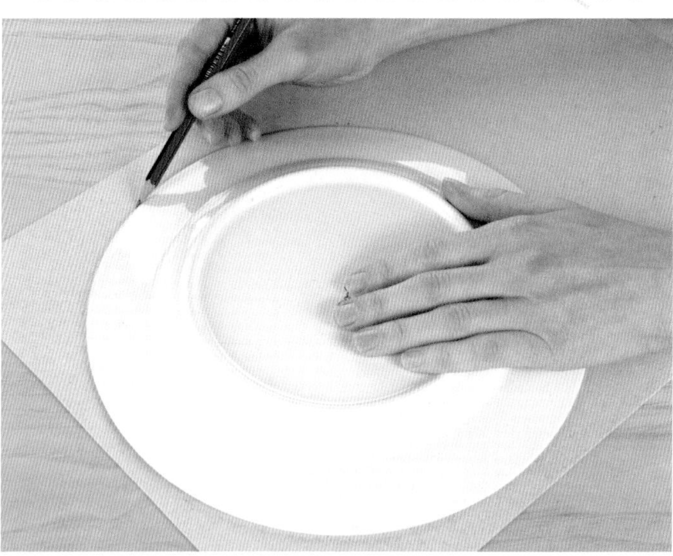

1 Start by drawing around a large dinner plate onto a sheet of thick cardboard. Place a saucer in the centre of the circle and draw around it to make the frame aperture. Cut out the frame with scissors. Cut out the aperture with a craft knife. Lightly sand the outer and inner edges of the frame to smooth them.

2 Lay sheets of scrap paper or newspaper over your work-surface. Without diluting it, and using the paint quite sparingly, brush a coat of cream emulsion paint over the front and back of the frame and leave to dry.

3 From cardboard cut a square of backing board for the frame. The board should be about 4cm (1½in) wider and taller than the frame aperture. Paint one side of the backing board with cream emulsion paint, as before, and leave to dry.

Hint Make the frame to match a favourite photo. Start by assessing the size of the required aperture – you can make a square or rectangular frame if that's easier. Then work outwards, making sure the frame is wide enough to support the hearts.

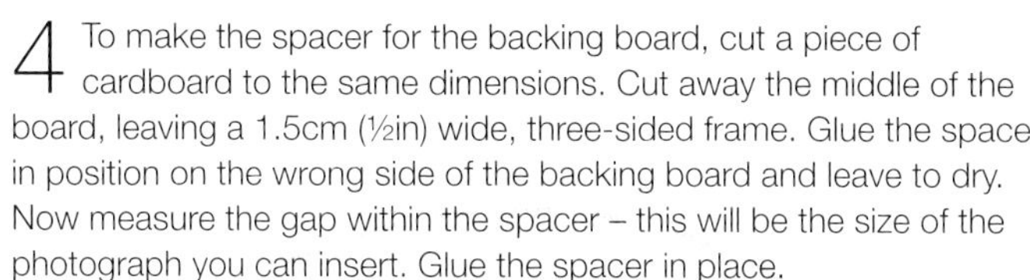

4 To make the spacer for the backing board, cut a piece of cardboard to the same dimensions. Cut away the middle of the board, leaving a 1.5cm (½in) wide, three-sided frame. Glue the spacer in position on the wrong side of the backing board and leave to dry. Now measure the gap within the spacer – this will be the size of the photograph you can insert. Glue the spacer in place.

5 Cut two small slits in the backing board about 2.5cm (1in) from the edge of the board without the spacer. Push split pins through the slits, from the front to the back, as shown. Open out the legs on the reverse of the board and tape over them to prevent them catching on the photograph.

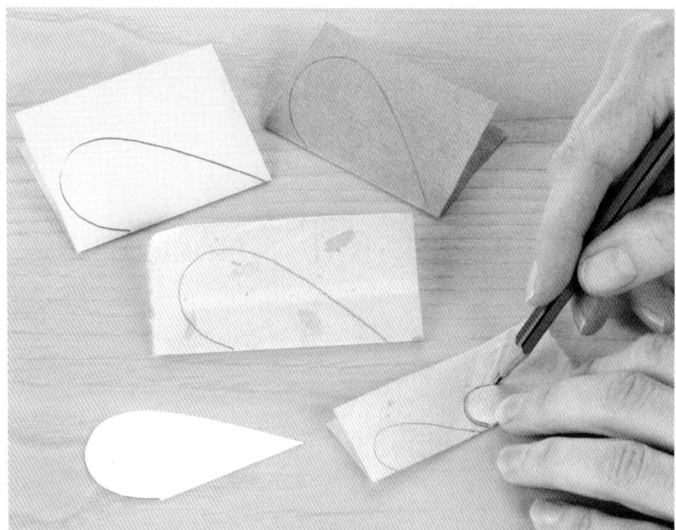

6 Trace and transfer the heart patterns from page 104 onto thin card to make templates. Cut out the templates with scissors, making sure the edges of the templates are smooth. Fold scraps of paper in various colours and patterns and place the template up to each fold; draw around the templates then cut out all the hearts.

7 Glue the large hearts in a circle around the frame, overlapping them at top and bottom. Glue the smaller hearts on top, resting them in the centres of the larger hearts. On the back of the frame, tie a length of cord to the heads of the split pins to make a hanger. Cut a photograph to the measurement you took in step 5 and slide it into the frame to finish.

Hanging Stars

Simple one-fold paper cuts are brilliant for making striking three-dimensional structures, like these festive hanging stars. The stars are cut individually for the sake of precision then stuck together in groups of four, six, eight or more. There is something very pleasing about the repetition of shape, and it is great fun to experiment with multiples of one-fold paper cuts to see what can be achieved from such a simple starting point.

Choosing the right paper is key to the success of this project. I have always loved Eastern European and Russian folk art, and their ornate Christmas decorations are particularly splendid, so these were the starting point for these paper creations.

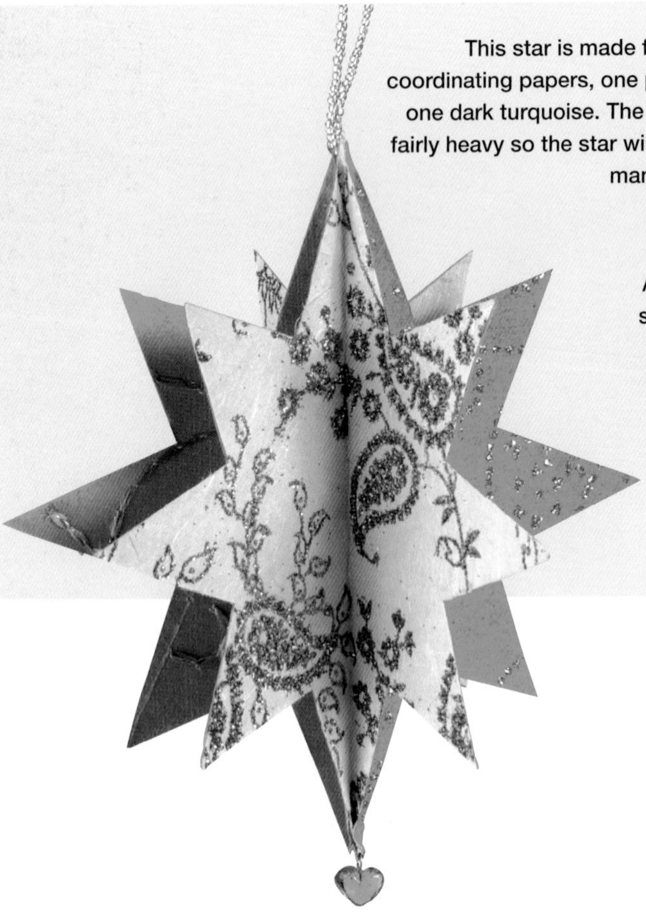

This star is made from two coordinating papers, one pale and one dark turquoise. The paper is fairly heavy so the star will last for many years.

A pendant bead secures the wire for the hanging loop, but it also adds an extra decorative touch and sparkles enticingly.

These splendid decorations are made from four, six or eight pieces so you don't have to use the same papers throughout. You could use one paper, two alternating papers or even use a different paper for each one. Instructions for making the bauble are provided on page 17.

Hanging Stars

you will need

- Eight A4 sheets of plain and/or patterned papers (see step 1)
- 28-gauge beading wire
- Flat-nose pliers
- Seed beads to coordinate with the paper
- Glass pendant bead to coordinate with the paper
- Basic tool kit

Hint Glue stick is ideal for sticking the stars together because it is easy to use and dries slowly enough to allow you time to position the sections together accurately. Paper clips can be used to hold the sections while the glue dries.

1 Trace the star pattern from page 105 and transfer it to thin card to make a template. Cut out the template with scissors. Fold the papers you wish to use in half – four plain and four different patterned papers were used here.

2 Place the template on the folded paper with the centre line of the template against the fold. Draw around the template to cut out eight stars, one at a time.

3 Spread glue on the backs of the stars, one half at a time. Butt the folded stars against each other, alternating plain and patterned papers, and matching the edges exactly. If necessary, place the completed star on a cutting mat, one face at a time, and trim away any excess paper with a craft knife.

4 Cut a 60cm (24in) length of 28-gauge beading wire. Thread a strand of seed beads approximately 20cm (8in) long onto the wire, as shown.

Inspiration

Experiment with the scale of your stars, and with the weight of paper used. Big stars cut from tissue paper in large multiples, of say, 16 or 32, would make fantastic room decorations at a Christmas party.

5 Position the beads in the centre of the wire and gently fold it in half to make a loop. Twist the excess wire beneath the beads to keep them in place.

6 Poke the free ends of the wire through the centre of the star. Gently pull the wire taut, until the loop of beads rests neatly on top of the star.

7 Thread the ends of the wire through the glass bead. Twist the ends of the wire together to keep the beaded loop taut. Don't pull too hard or the star will buckle out of shape. This bead should rest just below the star, as shown on page 14.

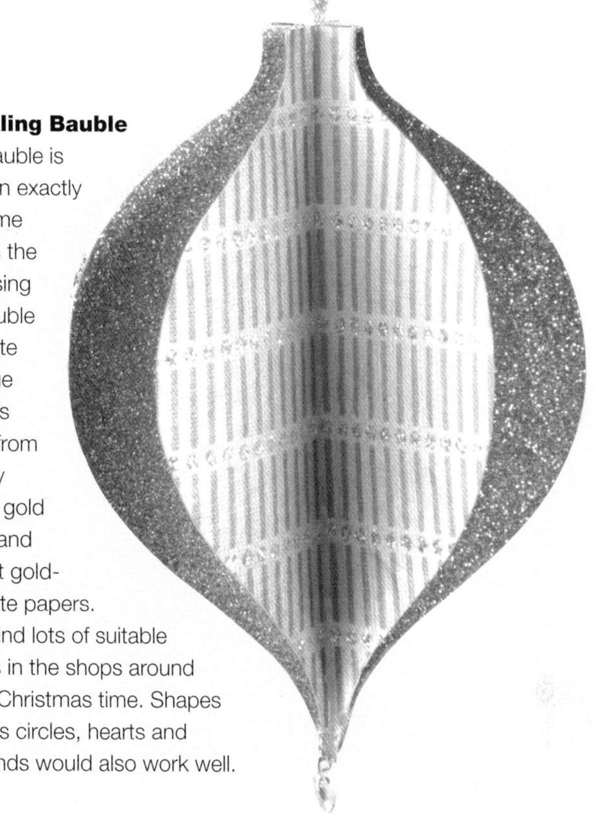

Sparkling Bauble
This bauble is made in exactly the same way as the star, using the bauble template on page 105. It's made from a lovely glittery gold paper and elegant gold-on-white papers. You'll find lots of suitable papers in the shops around about Christmas time. Shapes such as circles, hearts and diamonds would also work well.

Family-tree Album

A family tree is a popular motif, and this version is especially appealing because it has movement provided by the dangling picture leaves. It is designed to grace the cover of a family photo album but it would also make a brilliant picture to hang on the wall or a delightful three-dimensional keepsake (see the variation on page 23).

The design is based on the rose bush and urn forms that appear so frequently in folk art paper cuts, especially those of Poland. It also borrows another feature of Polish paper cutting – that of layering cut-out shapes on top of each other to produce a collaged effect. I have left the leaves dangling free from their threads, but you could glue them down.

The stunning cover of this scrapbook album shows what the book is all about – family. Let it set the high standard for the pages within.

A handy tie made from thin brown elastic has a leaf tag attached. The tie holds the album shut to help prevent accidental damage. If you like you can add your name, the date or subject of the album to the tag for easy reference.

Bring the concept of your family tree to life with this wonderful design, which would also work well on one of the pages of the album. Templates are provided for the tree and leaves, and these can easily be scaled up or down to suit the proportions of your family album.

Family-tree Album

you will need

- Photo album 30cm (12in) high
- A3 sheet of fairly thin dark green and warm brown handmade paper for the background and tree
- Scraps of brown and green handmade paper in several shades for the leaves
- Photos of the people you want to include on the cover
- 2.5cm (1in) circle punch
- Brown eyelet and fitting tools
- Thin linen thread
- Thin brown elastic
- Spray glue
- Basic tool kit

Hint Because the branches are fairly thin and the paper quite flimsy, cut out the tree with scissors rather than a craft knife, otherwise there is a chance the paper will tear.

1 Measure the front of the photo album. Cut a piece of green handmade paper to the same size and glue in place.

2 Trace the tree motif from page 106 and transfer it to thin card. Cut out the tree to make a template. Fold a piece of brown handmade paper in half. Place the tree template on the fold and draw around it. Cut out the tree and unfold.

3 Trace the leaf motifs from page 104 and use them to make templates as before. Fold small pieces of green and brown paper in half. Place all the leaf templates on the folds. Draw around them and cut out, then unfold.

Hint When punching out the photographs, slide each photograph into the punch upside down. Turn the punch over and position the picture so that the face falls exactly inside the circle. Then punch – it's that simple.

4 Use an eyelet punch to make a hole in the base of each leaf. Then cut ten 20cm (8in) lengths of brown linen thread. Tie a length of thread through each leaf, taking care not to crease the paper.

5 Cut each family member's face into a circle using a circle punch. Glue one person to each leaf.

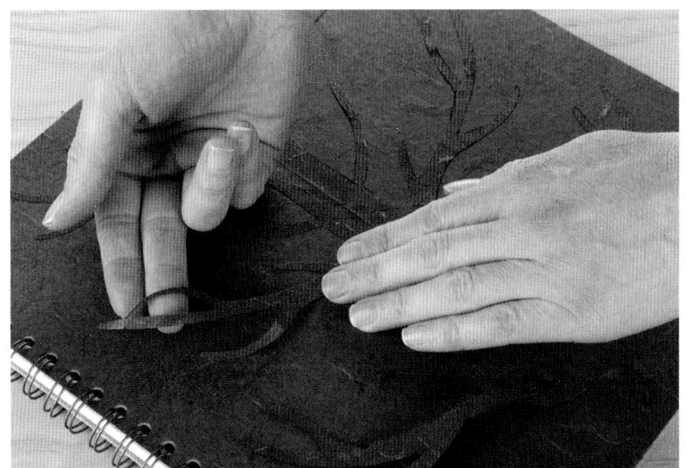

6 Spray glue onto the back of the tree. Position the tree centrally on the front of the photo album and lightly press into place. Move on to step 7 before the glue dries.

7 Lift each branch in turn. Push under the threads of each leaf to keep the leaf in place, with the photos facing outwards. Replace the branches and press firmly down onto the album.

Hint The hole in the leaf tag is reinforced with an eyelet so it won't tear when you stretch the elastic tie over the album. A brown eyelet picks up on the leaf colours.

8 Cut one more leaf from green paper. Glue it to thin card then cut it out. Punch a hole into the base of the leaf and insert an eyelet.

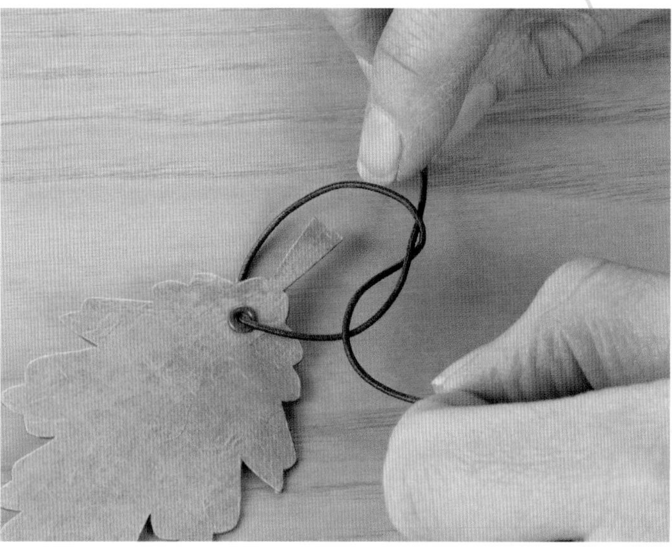

9 Thread the leaf onto thin brown elastic. Position it in the middle of the elastic and tie it in place.

10 Tie the elastic around the middle of the photo album, with the leaf in the centre. Tie the ends together at the back and cut away the excess elastic.

Inspiration

This doesn't have to be a family tree. Use it to show all the members of a club, team, class or group or to remember the people at a gathering, such as a reunion or wedding. Change the colours of the tree and leaves to suit the subject matter, using team colours for a football team, for example, or silver and white for a wedding day.

Friends Forever

You can adapt the family-tree idea very easily to make a friendship tree for children. Simply cut apples from red and green card and let your child stick pictures of their friends to the apples, writing their names underneath if they wish. Push a twig into a small, earth-filled plant pot and tie a leaf to each branch to complete the tree.

Garlands Galore

Whether strewn across ceilings, strung over doorways or windows, or used to decorate picture frames or other small items, there's something rather magical about paper garlands. You may have made Christmas garlands as a child, folding paper concertina style and then cutting out a motif through all layers at once – a thoroughly rewarding process because you create so much so quickly. Paper garlands are often associated with celebrations throughout the world.

As a portion of the folded edge at either side of the paper is left intact, the layers are still attached to each other when the concertina is opened out, forming a garland of connected shapes. As long as the left-hand side of the design makes sense when joined to the right in a long chain, anything can be depicted, whether symmetrical or not.

PREPARATION

Paper choice
Any weight of paper up to medium-weight (120-150gsm) can be used successfully for garlands. Handmade Japanese paper is especially pleasant to use. This is thin and easy to cut, but incredibly strong owing to the long fibres that are used in its manufacture, enabling you to make a lightweight but long-lasting garland.

Maintaining the joins
The most important thing to remember when cutting a garland is that part of the folded edges must be kept intact. If not, the garland will simply separate into individual sections once it is unfolded. To ensure this doesn't happen, measure the width of your template accurately, and fold your paper very slightly narrower.

TECHNIQUES

Pleating evenly
For accuracy, mark the width of the pleats along the top and bottom edge of both sides of the paper. Lightly score down between the first pair of marks, using an embossing tool or the back of a craft knife. Turn over the paper then score between the second set of marks. Repeat until all the lines are scored. Fold the paper along the score lines then flatten with a bone folder.

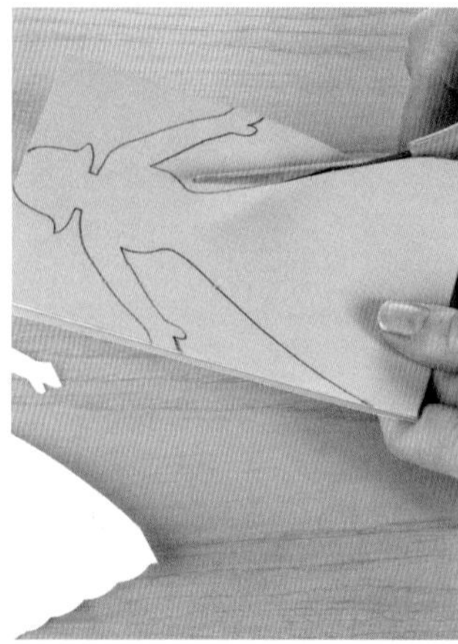

Cutting out the template
Place your template on the top pleat and draw around it, making sure the pencil lines extend right over the folds. Cut out your design, taking care not to snip through the side folds. Up to eight pleats of paper can be cut at once, but don't be tempted to cut more than this, as the layers will start to slide against each other, distorting the design.

Loving Album Card

Fill this five-page card with photos of happy memories – for an anniversary you could include pictures taken over the course of the marriage or for a birthday you could dig out embarrassing childhood images. You could even use it as a mini record of an event such as a wedding. Alternatively you could get friends and family to fill the pages with loving messages. It's ideal when lots of people want to sign the card.

- A2 sheet of medium-weight red paper
- A4 sheet of red embroidered paper
- Scraps of thin silver, gold and red card
- Heart punch
- Eyelet punch and hammer
- 30cm (12in) of gold elastic
- Photos (optional) to decorate the pages
- Basic tool kit

1 Cut a 45 x 9cm (17½ x 3½in) rectangle of medium-weight red paper. Fold the paper concertina style every 9cm (3½in) to make a five-page album.

2 Trace the large and small heart motifs from page 104 and transfer them to thin card to make templates. Place the large heart template on the top page of the closed album, lining the edges of the heart up with the folds in the paper. Draw around the template then cut out the shape.

Hint You could add a photo to the front of the card too. For a wedding or anniversary a portrait of the couple would work well, perhaps cut in a circle or heart shape.

3 Use the same template to cut two hearts from red embroidered paper. Glue one to the front and the other to the back of the album.

4 Transfer the smaller heart template onto thin silver card and cut it out. Punch three hearts from gold, red and silver card. Punch holes in all four hearts with an eyelet punch. String them onto a length of gold elastic and tie the elastic around the album to fasten it. Now add your photos or other embellishments.

Wedding Garland

A wedding provides the perfect opportunity to show off your paper-cutting skills, but because there is often so much to do at these times, this design is wonderfully simple so you won't need to spend weeks on the project. It is inspired by the whimsical Valentines of the Victorian era, and is light and ethereal in mood, perfect for a summer wedding.

The paper complements the elegant design and the importance of the occasion – it is heavy-weight handmade Japanese paper, which adds a luxurious look. Even using this strong paper you can easily cut most of the design with scissors and you can switch to a craft knife to remove the interior areas of waste paper.

The handmade Japanese paper used here has a translucent finish that adds to the delicate look of this garland, yet the paper is actually both strong and durable due to the long fibres used in its construction.

The rings are highlighted with gold tissue paper and the horseshoes in silver for added embellishment.

What a wonderful way to decorate a room for a wedding. Made from luxurious Japanese paper, the garland adds a real touch of class. The design could also be reduced on a photocopier and used to make name cards for the guests.

Wedding Garland

you will need

- Two A2 sheets of white handmade Japanese paper
- Gold and silver tissue paper
- Bradawl or large needle (optional)
- Eyelet tool
- Basic tool kit

Hint This garland would look wonderful placed around the edge of the main table at the wedding feast.

1 Cut four 20cm (8in) wide strips down the length of the paper. Pleat them into 12.5cm (5in) wide concertina folds – you should have four full pleats and a partial pleat on each piece.

2 Trace the dove and hearts pattern from page 107. Place the tracing face down onto one folded paper. Line up both sides of the tracing with the folded edges of the paper. Draw over the lines to transfer the design.

3 Place the folded paper on a cutting mat. Cut out all the interior areas with a craft knife, as shown, then cut around the outside of the design with scissors.

4 Keep the paper-cut folded and place it on a cutting mat. If desired, use a bradawl or needle to prick decorative dots into the paper in the positions indicated on the pattern. Repeat steps 2–4 for each folded strip.

Inspiration

The dove design is perfect for adaptation and can easily be used to produce related items of wedding stationery. For example, it could be cut from thin pearlescent card as a lovely invitation.

Hint If you find it fiddly sticking the gold and silver tissue paper in place, you can simply use a thick gold pen to colour in the rings and a silver pen for the horseshoes instead.

5 Pleat lengths of gold and silver tissue paper into 3cm (1¼in) wide concertina folds. Trace the rings and horseshoe motifs. Place the horseshoe tracing on the silver paper and the rings on the gold. Draw over the lines to transfer the motifs and cut them out.

6 Unfold the white paper cuts to reveal the garland. Spread a little glue on the back of each ring or horseshoe motif and stick it in place on the garland. When the glue is dry, carefully trim away any excess paper with a craft knife.

7 Cut small circles of gold tissue paper using an eyelet tool and glue them to the birds' heads to make eyes.

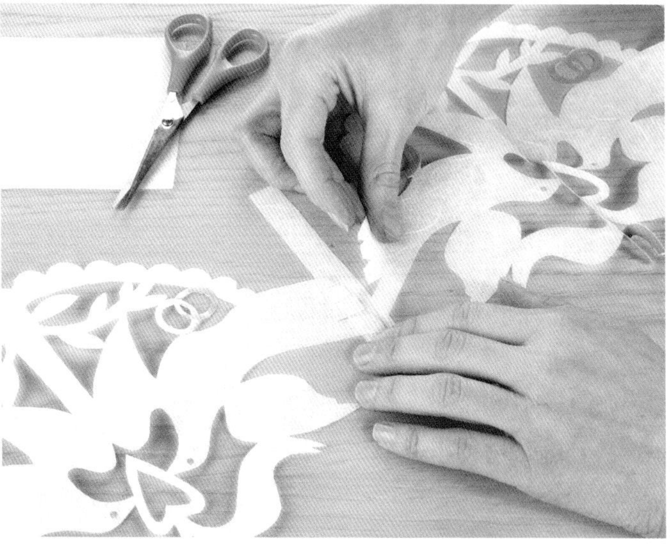

8 To join the strips of garland together first place them face down, with the tail feathers aligned. Cut a thin strip of paper and glue it over the join. Leave to dry. Trim away the excess paper then crease the join. Now your garland is ready to hang.

New Baby Garland

Made from thin card, this delightful pram garland is designed to stand on a mantelpiece or shelf. What a great way to welcome a baby home for the first time or to add a personal touch to his or her room. The garland is yellow with details in pink and blue so it will suit a boy or a girl, but if you like you could make it all blue, all pink or a bolder colour such as red or purple.

The garland is decorated in all sorts of ways with overlays of paper and punched shapes so as well as producing a lovely item you'll learn some very handy techniques that you can adapt for your other paper crafting projects. For example, the punched daisy wheels are attached with eyelets so they'll actually rotate.

The top of each pram is embellished with strips of patterned paper that have been cut with scallop-edge scissors to enhance the dainty design. The scallop works especially well here, but if you have other types of decorative-edge scissors you could experiment with them to see what you like best.

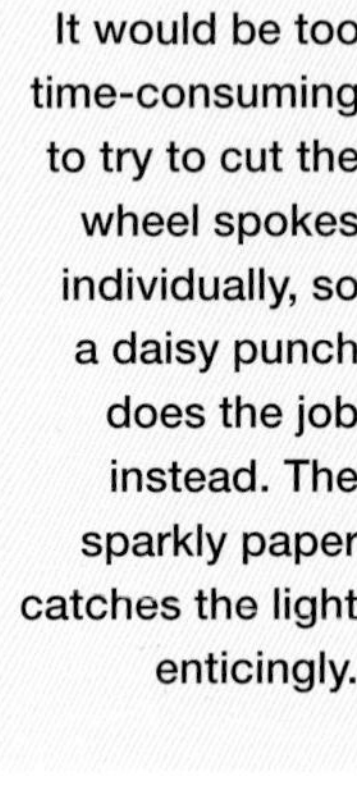

It would be too time-consuming to try to cut the wheel spokes individually, so a daisy punch does the job instead. The sparkly paper catches the light enticingly.

This enchanting garland fits perfectly along a mantelpiece as a 'welcome home' banner for a new baby. It could also be a spectacular card from family or friends.

New Baby Garland

you will need

- A2 sheet of lightweight pale yellow card
- A4 sheets of pale blue and pale pink plain and patterned papers
- A4 sheets of plain white, lilac, purple and silver paper
- Scallop-edge scissors
- Daisy punch
- Eyelet punch and setter
- Eyelets in pale pink and pale blue
- Basic tool kit

Inspiration

This idea could easily be adapted to form a mini album in which to record the first year of a child's life. Add photographs and personal details and even mementoes such as the hospital name tag.

1 Trace the pram template from page 108. Cut a 13.5cm (5¼in) wide strip of yellow card down the length of the A2 yellow card. Score and fold the yellow strip into five equal sections. Place the tracing on the paper, lining up the edges with the folds in the paper and transfer the design to the paper.

2 Cut around the outside of the pram with scissors and carefully cut out the inside areas between the wheels using a craft knife on a cutting mat.

3 Open out the garland. Glue a piece of plain pink or blue paper to the front of each pair of pram hoods. Carefully trim away the excess paper from around the hoods on the back of the garland.

4 Use scallop-edge scissors to cut a 6mm (¼in) wide strip of white paper to fit down the side of each hood. Glue in place. Cut 11.5cm (4½in) strips 6mm (¼in) wide from decorative paper and glue a strip just below each hood, covering the end of each white strip.

Hint If you have some medium-sized punches you could use one of these to cut the motif on the side of each pram instead of cutting the hearts by hand. You could use a heart, star, teddy or any other design that fits the theme.

5 Trace the heart template from page 108 and transfer it to coloured papers to match each hood (or see the hint above). Cut out the hearts and glue one to each pram.

6 Using a small and a medium coin as templates, cut out 20 small circles from lilac paper and 20 medium circles from purple paper. Glue a purple circle to each pram wheel then stick a lilac circle on top. Trim away any excess yellow paper from around the wheels.

7 To make the wheel spokes, punch 20 daisies from silver paper. Punch a hole in the centre of each one with an eyelet punch. Punch a corresponding hole in the centre of each wheel.

8 Attach each daisy to the centre of a wheel with an eyelet setter, using an eyelet in the same colour as the pram hood.

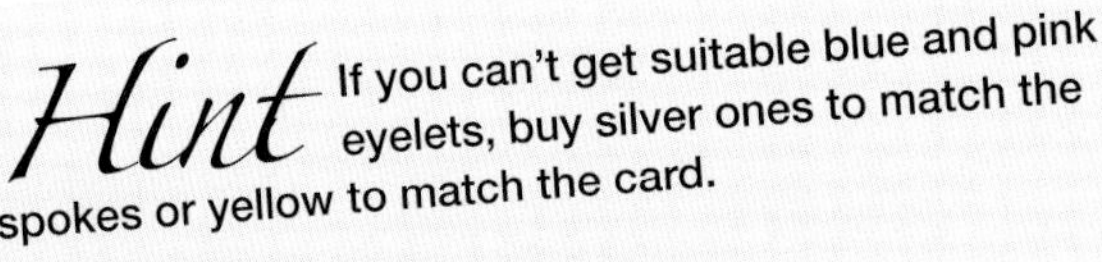

Hint If you can't get suitable blue and pink eyelets, buy silver ones to match the spokes or yellow to match the card.

Pirate Pennants

These piratical pennants make the perfect decoration for a young boy's bedroom. Inspired by Mexican fiesta flags, the pennants are created in bright colours. They can be attached to each other in groups or cut into single pennants and glued together, alternating the colours. A girl's version, featuring fairytale motifs cut from lilac, purple and pink, is shown on page 39.

You won't need many materials for this project – just some colourful tissue paper, scissors with a zigzag edge and your usual paper-cutting tools. If you don't already have the tissue paper, you could experiment with other lightweight papers, but otherwise you'll find the addition of tissue paper to your paper stash won't go amiss because it's got hundreds of uses.

Another term for pirate is buccaneer, that sword-flashing adventurer of the Spanish Main, so here's a motif for him.

This skull-and-crossbone design says it all – pirates abound. It has a naïve look that's bound to appeal to children but it is complicated enough to demand your concentration when cutting out.

These piratical pennants set the scene for some serious dressing-up fun. If you've got other pirate-themed accessories to go with them, you can easily copy some of the designs onto additional pennants for a coordinated effect.

Pirate Pennants

you will need

34 x 50cm (13½in x 20in) pieces of tissue paper in blue, red and yellow (each piece makes four pennants)

Pinking shears or paper scissors with a zigzag decorative edge

Basic tool kit

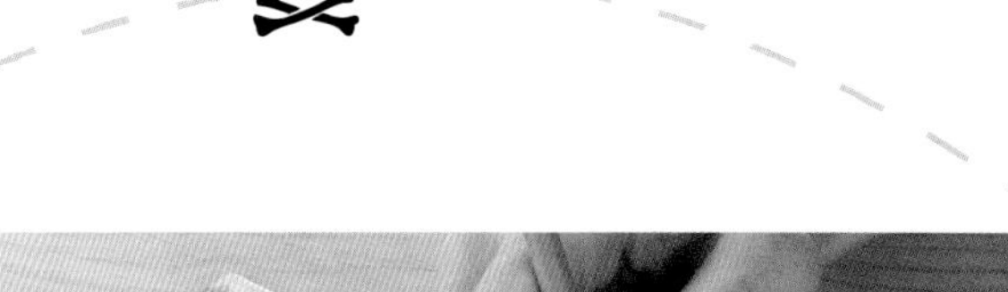

1 To make four flags in the same colour, fold a 34 x 50cm (13½in x 20in) rectangle of tissue paper in half and then in half again.

2 Draw an equilateral triangle on the paper, making it as large as possible and finishing the end of the triangle 4cm (1½in) from one short side, as shown.

3 Cut along the sides of the triangle using pinking shears or decorative scissors with a zigzag edge. Keep the four layers close together so you can cut accurately.

4 Trace the anchor and star patterns from page 109 and transfer them to the triangular flag, centring the design on the paper and using the photograph on page 35 as your guide.

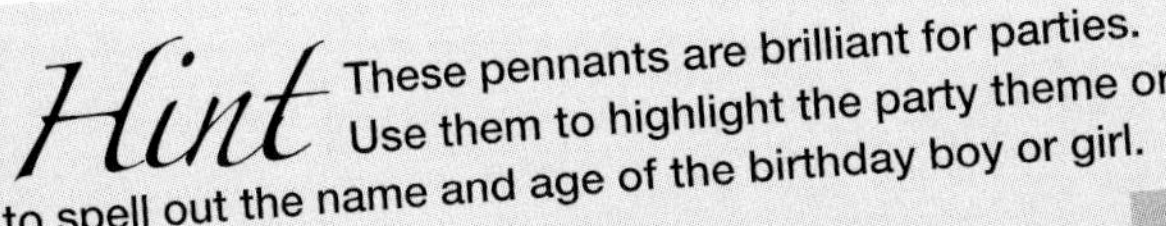
Hint These pennants are brilliant for parties. Use them to highlight the party theme or to spell out the name and age of the birthday boy or girl.

5 Place the paper on a cutting mat and cut out the pattern carefully with a craft knife.

6 Trim off the very top of the paper, as close to the fold as possible, to separate the pairs of flags.

7 Repeat, using other colours and designs (see the templates on page 109) to make as many flags as you require. To assemble the flags, line up the sections and fold up the edges by approximately 1cm (½in).

8 Glue the edges together then turn over the edge and press the fold down gently with your fingers to flatten it. Leave to dry before hanging up the pennants.

The lower edges of the pennants are shapes with zigzag scissors, though you could cut them with ordinary scissors, if preferred, or use any decorative-edge scissors that you have in your tool kit.

The girl's garland is decorated with small dots of silver glitter glue for extra sparkle. You can add highlights to the boy's garland in the same way, if desired, with gold touches on the sword, for example, or silver on the anchor motif.

Inspiration

Adapt this idea to suit your child's favourite theme. Cut from inexpensive tissue paper, these pennants can be changed as often as the ideas of your child's imagination.

To make a garland for a little girl, choose pastel-coloured tissue paper and fairytale motifs. There are three designs fit for a princess, all combined with a pretty heart border – a slipper, a crown and a fairytale castle. You'll find the templates, which should be enlarged by 200%, on page 109.

Paper Lace

Intricate and delicate, paper lace can be astoundingly detailed or relatively simple and graphic. It is always symmetrical. The paper is folded before it is cut, and sometimes it is folded several times vertically, horizontally or even diagonally. For variety, the paper can be cut in a circle or other shape and folded several times to create wonderful kaleidoscopic designs, snowflakes and the like.

Paper lace appears as an art form in many cultures, including those of Latin America, Asia and Eastern Europe. In Poland, pictorial depictions of weddings, farming scenes and everyday life are known as Wycinanki, while snowflake forms are called Gwiazdy, Polish for 'stars' (see page 42 for a snowflake project). In the United States and Western Europe, the techniques were traditionally used to make paper doilies and mats, and Valentine's cards were very popular too.

TOOLS AND MATERIALS

Perfect paper
As with all folded paper cuts, anything up to medium-weight paper is suitable. A higher weight will not only be tricky to fold neatly, but it will be difficult to cut through two layers at once.

Hint **Once you've traced a complex design onto paper, tint the areas to be cut away by lightly scribbling over them with pencil. That way, you won't cut out the wrong bit by mistake and ruin your hard work.**

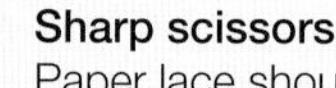

Sharp scissors
Paper lace should be cut out very carefully using sharp scissors and a craft knife, if desired. Although embroidery scissors are very sharp, the short blades tend to leave a jagged edge around the paper. I prefer to use pointed paper-craft scissors with longer blades, as they make long, smooth cuts. If you don't feel confident with a craft knife you can use your scissors to cut away interior shapes. First pierce a hole in the centre of the area to be cut away using the tips of the blades then insert the scissors into the hole and start cutting.

TECHNIQUES

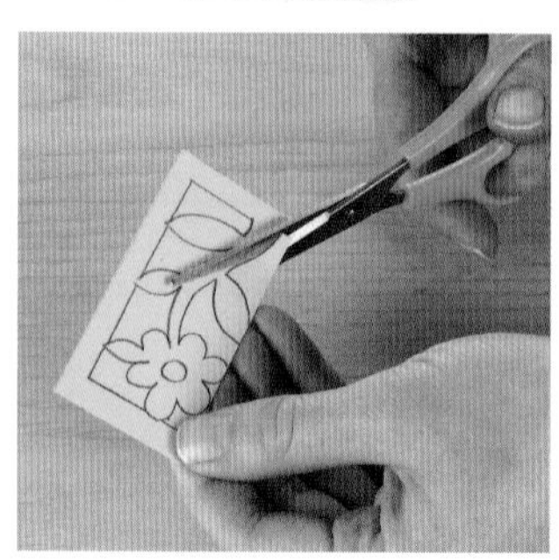

1 When cutting out a traced design aim to turn the paper rather than your scissors as you follow the pencil line so that you feed the paper smoothly through the blades. Cut around the motif from the edge of the paper as far along the pencil line as possible until it changes direction.

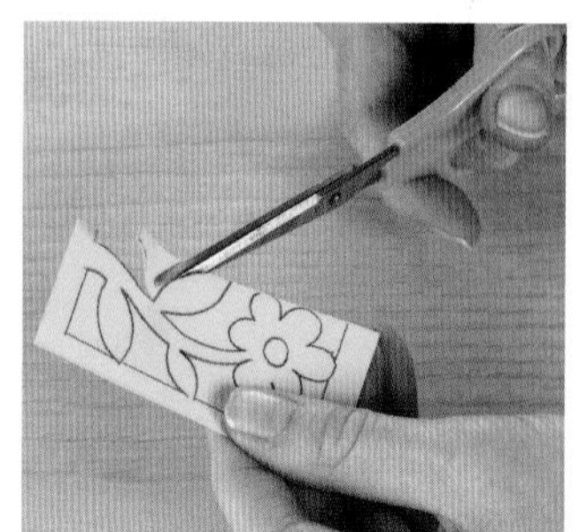

2 Now remove your scissors and cut towards the same point from another direction, as shown. If you try to change direction or cut around tight curves without removing your scissors, you run the risk of snagging or creasing your paper.

Lacy Flower Card

This graphic card design is ideal for teenagers and hard-to-please adults alike. Its bold brown, blue and pink colour combination enhances the simple yet striking design of the flowers. What's more, it's quick and easy to make – the flowers are just circles folded into quarters and then cut with simple designs, and additional embellishments are provided with strips and circles of paper plus some pretty sequins.

you will need

- 29 x 14.5cm (11½ x 5¾in) rectangle of cream card folded in half to make a 14.5 x 14.5cm (5¾ x 5¾in) card blank
- Scraps of chocolate brown, blue, blue patterned, raspberry pink and lime green paper
- Pair of compasses
- Silver and blue flower sequins
- Basic tool kit

1 Glue a 7.5 x 14.5cm (3 x 5¾in) rectangle of brown paper to the lower half of the card. Glue a 7.5 x 8.5cm (3 x 3¼in) rectangle of blue plain paper to the top left-hand corner and a 1.5cm (½in) strip of blue patterned paper over the join.

2 Cut one 7cm (2¾in) circle of pink paper. Cut three 5cm (2in) circles from pink, blue patterned and brown paper. Fold all the circles into quarters. Trace the flower patterns from page 104 and transfer them to the circles. Cut out and unfold.

Hint **Instead of cutting strips of paper for embellishment you could use fabric or paper ribbon. Paper ribbons, designed for card-making, can be sticky-backed, making them quick and easy to apply.**

3 Glue a scrap of coloured paper to the back of each flower to make the decorative centres. Punch a dot from lime green paper and glue it to the centre of the large flower. Glue the flowers to the card.

4 Glue a thin strip of pink paper across the middle and lower edge of the card. Cut a thin strip of brown paper and glue it to the right-hand side of the blue paper. Glue sequins along the centre band.

Snowflake Tea Lights

Inspired by the wonderful Polish paper cuts, called Gwiazdy, that are made in the Lowicz region of Poland, these tea lights are decorated with elegant, fine-lined paper snowflakes. The designs are simple and surprisingly quick to cut, and the process is strangely addictive, so you may soon find yourself experimenting to invent your own snowflake designs.

Tissue paper is used for the snowflakes because it is thin enough to lie smoothly against the outside of the glass and because of its translucency – when the candlelight shines through, it illuminates the colour, giving it the appearance of stained glass.

For added glitter, the centre and tips of each snowflake have been embellished with a stick-on clear glass stone. If you can't get hold of these, you could use sequins instead or tiny punched shapes cut from holographic paper.

There are three snowflake designs to choose from, or you could go for something altogether different, like the Halloween motifs on page 45.

Tea-light holders magnify the light from the candle and protect it from any breezes that might either extinguish it or make it burn too quickly. These delicate snowflake designs won't obscure the light but they will add to the atmosphere and enhance your wintry theme.

Snowflake Tea Lights

you will need

Glass tea-light holder
Scraps of white and pale blue tissue paper
Zigzag scissors
Spray glue
Self-adhesive clear glass stones
Basic tool kit

1 Wash the tea-light holder to remove any traces of grease and dirt then dry thoroughly. Use zigzag scissors to cut two thin strips of tissue paper, about 4mm (⅛in) wide.

2 Lightly spray the back of the strips with glue then position one around the top and the other around the bottom edge of the tea-light holder. Smooth them into place to make decorative bands then trim off the excess paper at the join.

3 Cut a 5cm (2in) diameter circle from tissue paper. Fold it in half, then in half twice more.

4 Trace a snowflake design from page 110 lightly onto the folded tissue paper, taking care to extend the pencil lines right up to each side of the paper, as shown.

Inspiration

The tissue-paper snowflakes can be attached to windows with a little spray glue to make a temporary festive decoration, while if they are cut from heavier paper, they make lovely Christmas-tree decorations, especially enhanced with a sprinkling of glitter.

5 Cut away the excess paper from the snowflake using small, sharp scissors. Now you can open out the snowflake to reveal the finished design.

6 Lightly spray the back of the snowflake with glue then position it on the front of the tea-light holder between the zigzag bands. Smooth it into place. Finally, stick on a small glass stone at the end of each point of the star as a sparkling accent and add a final stone at the centre.

Spooky Trio
This idea is easily adapted. Here are three fantastic Halloween designs, which are cut from unfolded tissue paper. The motifs are taken from the Halloween window design, the templates for which are on page 111. Enlarge them to fit the tea-light holder.

Inspiration

You could also make Christmas versions with tree or snowman motifs, or birthday tea-light holders with a cake and candle motif or the number of the birthday – the options are endless.

Chinese Chandelier

Deceptively simple to make, this paper chandelier makes an unusual and colourful interior decoration. If you make several in festive colours they could be hung at Christmas, and you could also make tiny versions to hang on the tree. The design is inspired by Chinese fretwork and is assembled from three separate lace cuts. The chandelier is finished with simple paper tassels made from fringed tissue.

To make the chandelier shown you will need some A3 sheets of thin card in pink and red plus an equally large sheet of card to make the template. The tassels are made from coordinating tissue paper, though vellum could also work well.

As the chandelier turns, the sizzling contrast between the bold red and bright pink comes into play.

The more you study this delicate chandelier, the more details you will notice, such as the pretty butterfly and flower motifs.

Add an exotic touch to your living room or dining room with this sumptuous chandelier. The red and pink combination is bright and exotic but gold and black could be equally gorgeous.

Chinese Chandelier

you will need

- A3 sheet of thin card to make the template
- A3 sheet of thin pink card
- Two A3 sheets of thin red card
- Orange tissue paper: three 15 x 10cm (6 x 4in) rectangles
- Pink tissue paper: two 15 x 10cm (6 x 4in) rectangles and one 15 x 14cm (6 x 5½in) rectangle
- Red tissue paper: one 15 x 10cm (6 x 4in) rectangle and one 15 x 14cm (6 x 5½in) rectangle
- Paper glue, such as stick adhesive
- Clothes' pegs
- Red satin embroidery thread
- 50cm (20in) length of 3mm (⅛in) wide red satin ribbon
- 50cm (20in) length of 10mm (⅜in) wide red satin ribbon
- Basic tool kit

1 Enlarge and trace the chandelier pattern from page 111 and transfer it to thin white card to make a template. Cut it out carefully. Fold a sheet of thin pink card in half. Place the centre of the chandelier template on the fold as indicated on the template and draw around it onto the card.

Hint **If you have some lovely A4 sheets of thin card that you'd like to use for these decorations, simply photocopy the chandelier template at 125% instead of 200%. It should then fit neatly on folded A4 card and will be about 19cm (7½in) high.**

2 Carefully cut around the outside of the chandelier design on the pink card with scissors.

3 Cut out all the interior sections of the chandelier using a craft knife and working on a cutting mat.

4 Repeat the process twice more using folded red card, making sure that you place the template exactly on the fold.

5 Open out each chandelier section at right angles (90°). Align the three sections and secure them at top and bottom with clothes' pegs, as shown.

6 Match the sections together as precisely as you can, then carefully glue them together (though see the hint below). I used stick adhesive for this job. Leave to dry.

7 Place each section in turn on a cutting mat and carefully trim away any excess card.

Hint Leave the bottom of the lower 'arms' unstuck in step 6. This makes it easier to insert the ribbon holding the smaller tassels in step 13.

8 To make the smaller pink tassels, place one small pink tissue paper rectangle on top of a matching orange tissue-paper rectangle and fold in half.

9 Keeping the layers together, snip along the unfolded edge about every 3mm (⅛in) to within 1cm (⅜in) of the fold to create fringing.

10 Roll up the layers to make a tassel, taking care not to trap the fringed ends of the paper. Repeat, making one more pink and orange tassel and one red and orange tassel. Make one large tassel using the large red and pink rectangles of tissue paper.

11 Cut four 15cm (6in) lengths of satin embroidery thread. Wrap a length tightly around the top of each tassel and tie the ends.

12 Cut three 10cm (4in) lengths of thin satin ribbon. Fold them in half and glue the looped ends into the tops of the smaller tassels. Repeat for the larger tassel using a 15cm (6in) length of ribbon.

13 Gently pull apart a small section of the three lower 'arms' of the chandelier. Glue in the smaller tassel ribbons and trim. Tie the larger tassel to the base of the chandelier.

14 Finally, tie a length of wider satin ribbon through the loop at the top of the chandelier to suspend it.

Inspiration

This design could be made even more dramatic if six or even eight sections are glued together.

Halloween Window

Skeletons, witches and black cats dance across this spooky Halloween picture, which is designed as a window display and was inspired by the humorous Day of the Dead paper cuts from Mexico. The paper cut is made in black and it is backed with coloured tissue for a glorious stained-glass effect when the light shines through. The design is an impressive 35 x 50cm (13¾ x 19¾in), so it is large enough to fill a small window and encourage any passing Trick or Treaters to knock if they dare. Don't be put off by the scale of this design. A little planning and preparation will make it easier to produce good results.

Black paper is used for the paper cut to mimic the leading in stained glass and because this is the traditional colour used for cutting silhouettes.

Tissue paper, which is used for the backing, is like coloured glass, allowing some light to filter through and seeming to glow. You could use one colour for the backing, but it's more fun to combine several.

This wonderful design contains all the elements you could wish for in a Halloween picture: skeletons, ghosts, black cats, pumpkins and witches. They are all depicted in a wonderfully swaying fashion, which adds a quirky touch and a sense of movement. Children will love it.

Halloween Window

you will need

- A2 sheet of black paper
- Tissue paper in orange, red and lime green plus any other colours you wish to use
- White transfer paper
- White wax crayon
- Eyelet punch
- Hammer
- Basic tool kit

Hint Tissue paper tends to fade when exposed to sunlight, so using coloured plastic film or acetate instead of tissue paper to back the paper cut would make the colours last longer.

1 Cut a 35 x 50cm (13¾ x 19¾in) rectangle of black paper and fold it in half lengthways.

2 Trace the window design from page 111. Position the transfer paper face down on top of the black paper, lining up the left-hand side of the transfer paper with the fold in the black paper. Place the tracing on top. Draw over the lines to transfer the design.

3 Remove the tracing and transfer paper. To help prevent any mistakes, block in the areas of the design that are to be cut away using a white wax crayon.

Inspiration

You don't have to cut the whole picture – you could make just one area. For example, a skeleton cut out and backed with tissue paper in the same way would look great. You can easily enlarge the motif on a photocopier.

4 Place the black paper on a cutting mat. Use a craft knife to cut out all the detailed parts of the design first then remove the larger areas of waste paper using a knife and scissors.

5 Now use an eyelet punch to make the eyes on the smaller figures, such as the bats and the witch.

6 Referring to the photograph on page 53, trace the main panels of the design and transfer these shapes to sheets of orange, red and green tissue paper. Cut them out to make the panels then set them aside.

Hint If you like you can use lightweight card or fairly thick handmade paper for this design. A strong paper or thin card will make the finished window hanging more durable.

7 Pick out any details or areas that you want to emphasize by gluing tiny scraps of contrasting tissue paper to the back of the paper cut, for example over some of the skulls' eyes and witches' dresses. Finally, glue the large panels of tissue paper over the back of the paper cut.

One of a Kind

A one-of-a kind design cut from flat, unfolded, paper is perfect when you want to create impact or for an asymmetrical effect. The whole design could be created in this way or you might wish to use folding and cutting techniques for certain elements, such as a decorative border.

This method of cutting has been used for centuries. In Europe, a paper craft called Scherenschnitte developed in the 1800s, in which complex designs were cut freehand from paper using razor-sharp scissors. Around the same time paper silhouettes became very popular, with portraits cut in profile from black paper.

TOOLS

Paper and card
For these designs, medium-weight (190gsm) watercolour paper or handmade paper is ideal because it is sturdy enough to withstand intricate cutting but is soft enough to cut easily with a blade. Thin card also works well, especially if you are making a carousel, but it is more difficult to cut, and you will need to replace your blade more frequently.

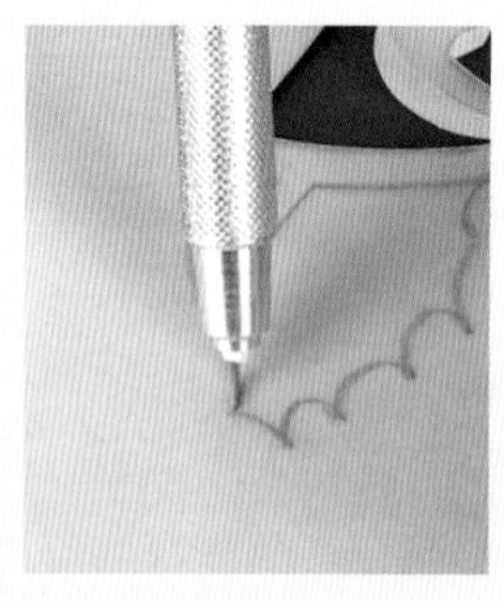

Knife with rotating blade
If I am cutting a very complex design I use a knife with a rotating blade. This has a small blade that swivels 360° to allow for extra precision around intricate curves. As with all types of craft knives, replace the blade as soon as it starts to blunt to ensure you cut cleanly, without tearing the paper.

TECHNIQUES

Making multiple cuts
Save time by cutting several designs at once. To do this, cut several pieces of paper to the same size and place in a stack. Hold the corners together with tiny dots of sticky putty, such as Blu-Tack, and attach the tracing to the top sheet. Transfer the design by drawing over the pencil lines then cut out as usual.

Using spray glue
A finished paper cut is fragile and easily torn so to attach it to the background use spray glue, which doesn't require dragging over the surface with an applicator as with other glue types. Hold the can at least 20cm (8in) away and spray lightly, taking several sweeps of spray as required.

Card of Peace

Try out this technique on a small project like this stunning dove card. The design is cut in medium-weight watercolour paper and then mounted onto blue card that suggests a summer sky. A small red punched heart is added to its beak for a romantic note. This kind of design gives a good opportunity to refine your cutting techniques because there are some intricate curves to contend with.

you will need

- 17.5 x 15cm (7 x 6in) rectangle of medium-weight white watercolour paper
- Scrap of red paper
- 17.5 x 30cm (7 x 12in) rectangle of thin blue card
- Small heart punch
- Basic tool kit

Hint **Need an envelope? This card will fit inside the fringed envelope bag featured on page 94.**

1 Trace the dove pattern from page 110 onto tracing paper. Place the tracing face down on the watercolour paper, matching the corners carefully, and redraw the design lines to transfer the design to the paper.

2 Place the watercolour paper on a cutting mat and carefully cut away all the excess paper from around the design.

3 Fold the rectangle of thin blue card in half to make a 17.5 x 15cm (7 x 6in) card blank. Lightly spray the back of the paper cut with glue and stick it to the front of the card blank.

4 Punch a heart from a scrap of red paper. Glue the heart to the card as a finishing touch so that it just touches the dove's beak.

Carousel Mobile

Whether hanging from the ceiling of a young child's room or standing on an item of furniture, this colourful mobile is bound to please. It's made from medium-weight card for strength and embellished with paper scraps, and you could add even more details, if desired, using paper, stick-on gems, glitter and so on. There are lots of details to apply, but because they are cut out separately, if you do make a mistake you can simply remake that element. If desired, you can add more horses to make the carousel larger, extending the length of yellow card to accommodate them. To prevent your work of art being damaged, hang it up well out of the reach of small hands, as this is a design that every child will wish to examine in detail.

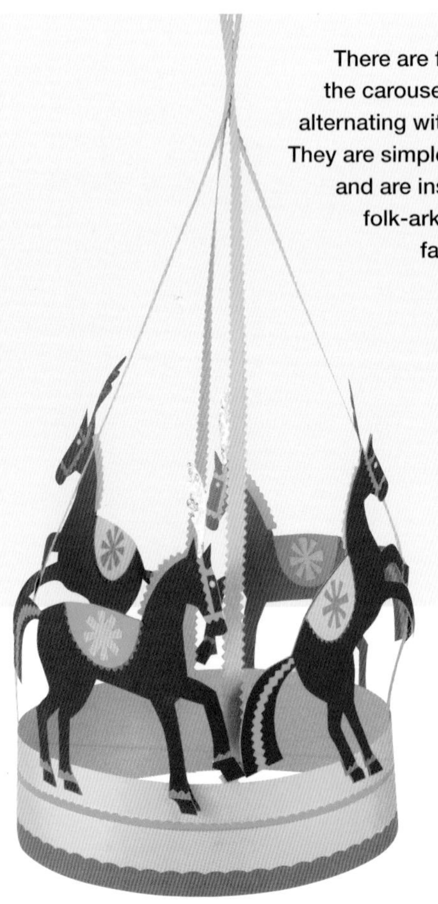

There are four horses on the carousel, two walking alternating with two rearing. They are simple and stylized, and are inspired by rural folk-ark paper cuts of farming scenes.

Zigzag scissors are brilliant for adding decorative detail to craft projects in no time. Here they have been used to make the horses' bridles, for example.

Any child will be inspired by this captivating mobile with its colourful combination of yellow, purple, red and blue that conjures up all the fun of the fair. The walking and rearing horses seem to have a movement of their own, which will be enhanced when the mobile sways in air.

Carousel Mobile

you will need

- A2 sheet of medium-weight purple card
- A2 sheet of medium-weight yellow card
- A2 sheets of red and blue card
- Scraps of pink, orange and gold paper
- 2.5cm (1in) diameter circle punch (optional)
- Zigzag scissors
- Wide and narrow scallop-edge scissors
- Eyelet punch
- Basic tool kit

Hint A sticker maker may be a useful investment if you wish to stick on lots of small pieces of paper, such as the bridles. You simply run paper or card through the machine and it puts a sticky layer on the back plus a protective backing.

1 Trace the horse pattern from page 112 and transfer it to purple card. Cut out the horses. Now trace and transfer the saddle pattern to yellow and blue card. Cut out the saddles, two for each horse, and glue them all to red card. Trim closely around the curve of the saddles with zigzag scissors.

2 To make stars for the saddles, cut or punch circles of pink and orange paper, 2.5cm (1in) in diameter. Fold the circles into quarters and snip where marked. Unfold the stars and glue them to the saddles. Glue the saddles to the fronts and backs of the horses.

3 Cut 1cm (⅜in) wide strips of pink, orange, blue and red paper with zigzag scissors. Cut them in half to make thin strips and glue them to the fronts and backs of the horses' heads to make bridles. Glue short strips to the fronts of the horses' ankles as decoration.

Inspiration

This kind of carousel mobile is very adaptable and could feature any kind of animal or small figures, depending on your taste. You could change the colour scheme to match a child's bedroom, or dispense with the hanging strips altogether and have it as a freestanding ornament.

4 Draw around the horses' necks onto coloured paper and cut out with straight and zigzag scissors to make manes. Trace and transfer the horses' headdresses to gold paper. Cut out the headdresses. Glue the manes and headdresses to the horses.

5 Punch small circles of paper for the eyes and glue them in place. Cut curves of coloured paper with zigzag scissors and glue to the fronts and backs of the horses' tails. Cut a band of yellow paper 6.5cm (2½in) wide and 75cm (30in) long. Glue the horses' feet to the band, about 2cm (¾in) down from the top edge.

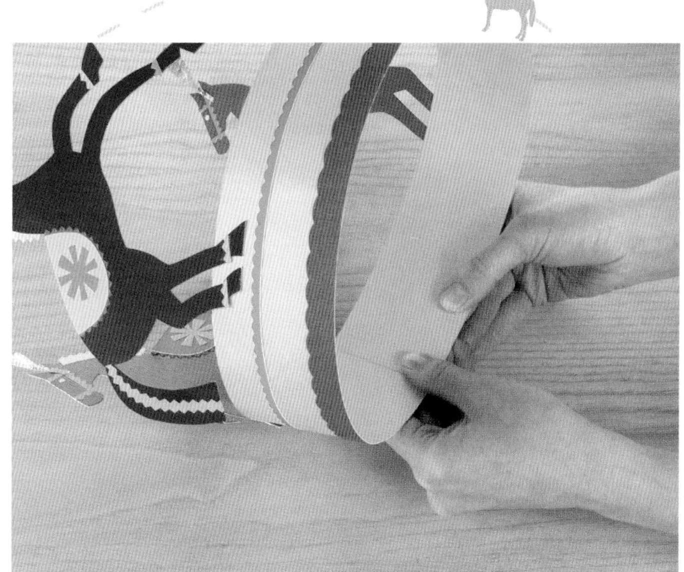

6 Cut a 2cm (¾in) wide strip of red card to fit along the yellow band. Cut a wide scallop edge along one side of the strip then glue it along the bottom of the band. Cut a 5mm (⅛in) strip the same length from blue card with narrow scallop-edge scissors. Glue above the red strip, just below the horses' hooves. When the glue is dry, curve the yellow band around in a circle and glue the ends together, overlapping by about 5cm (2in).

7 Finally, cut four 1cm (⅜in) wide strips of yellow card 50cm (20in) long, with zigzag scissors. Glue the strips between the horses and join them in a loop at the top to make the hanger.

Festive Table Runner

This cheerful Christmas runner, with its characterful folk-art motifs, is sure to be the centrepiece of your Christmas festivities. In fact, it's so lovely that you may not want to risk putting it on the table at all, but could frame it instead as a lasting Christmas decoration. It is more of a challenge than previous projects because of the fine detailing on the Christmas stockings, trees, buildings and so on but this detail brings an amazing vitality to the paper cut.

I was inspired to make it by the traditional Scherenschnitte paper cuts of Switzerland and Germany. For these, fantastically detailed, highly complex designs of domestic scenes, fairy tales, landscapes and the natural world were cut freehand from paper.

Fine detailing, as on the baubles, leaves and trees, adds to the magic of this project and shows the hand of a skilled craftsperson.

If you haven't the time for a large project like this, adapt the idea for a set of coasters – see page 67.

There is something especially lovely about Christmas decorations that are hand-made and that have clearly taken a lot of work. They pull us back to our roots and remind us that the best home embellishments are made, not bought. This classic design will be a treasured heirloom in years to come.

Festive Table Runner

you will need

- Roll of red Kraft paper
- Roll of white Kraft paper
- Small paintbrush for applying glue
- Swivel knife such as a Coluzzle knife and appropriate mat, if required
- Rubber roller
- Basic tool kit

Hint **A rotating knife makes it easier to cut the fine details, like the twists on this tree, but it takes practice to use it properly. If you haven't used one before, try it on a smaller project first or use an ordinary craft knife or very sharp, slender scissors and take your time.**

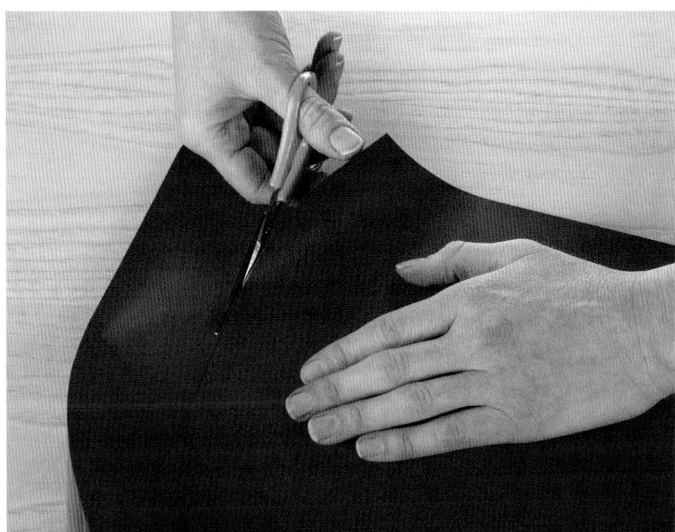

1 Decide how long you want your table runner to be: either the same length as your table end-to-end or longer, to overlap the sides. Cut a piece of red paper 40cm (16in) wide and as long as you require. Cut a piece of white backing paper to the same size plus 10cm (4in) all round.

2 Trace all the runner templates from pages 114-115. Place them face down on the back of the runner and redraw over the lines to transfer the images. You can repeat some of the images, for example the trees and snowman, to fill the space as necessary.

3 Shade in all the areas of the design that you wish to keep (or remove) before you start to avoid cutting away the wrong part of the design.

Inspiration

The red and white colour combination is typically Scandinavian and suits the Christmas theme, but you could use green and white or any other festive colours that suit your room scheme.

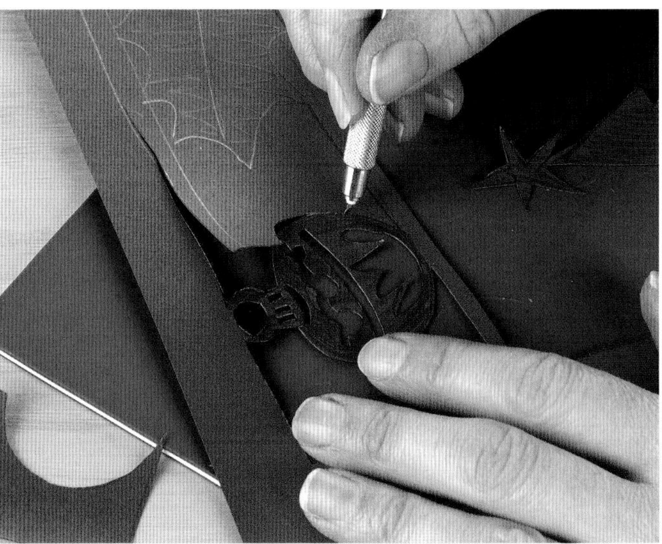

4 Place the runner on a cutting mat. Working on the main panel first, cut out all the small details, such as the roof tiles, tree decorations and stocking patterns first. Once the details are completed, cut away the paper from around the main parts of the design, as shown.

5 Cut carefully around the stockings, stars, holly and bauble in the border at the top of the runner, making sure that they stay attached. A swivel knife makes this easier.

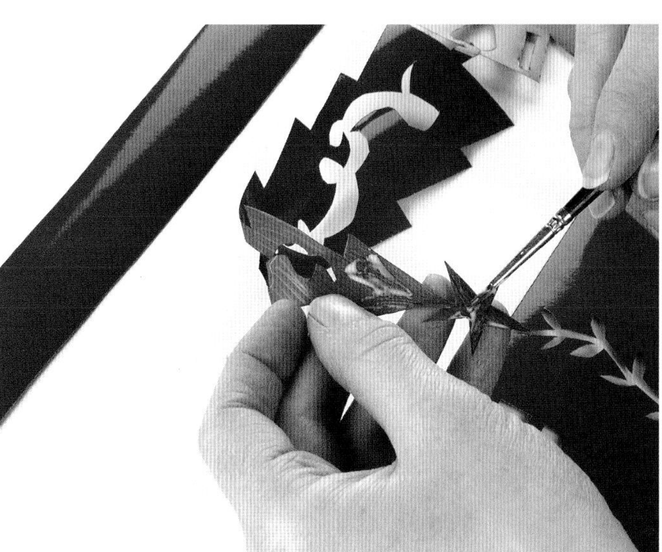

6 Slide the runner onto the length of white backing paper. Place it centrally and make sure that the runner is lying square and that the design is not distorted. Attach the corners of the runner to the paper with sticky putty such as Blu-Tack.

7 Lift one section of the paper cut at a time and apply PVA glue to the back with a small brush.

Hint **If you can't find rolls of Kraft paper, wallpaper or a long roll of plain gift-wrap make good alternatives.**

8 Drop the paper cut down onto the backing paper and pat it very gently into place using your fingertips. Take care not to wrinkle the paper cut or stretch it out of shape.

9 Once the paper cut is glued in position, carefully go over it with a rubber roller to bond it to the backing paper and remove any air bubbles.

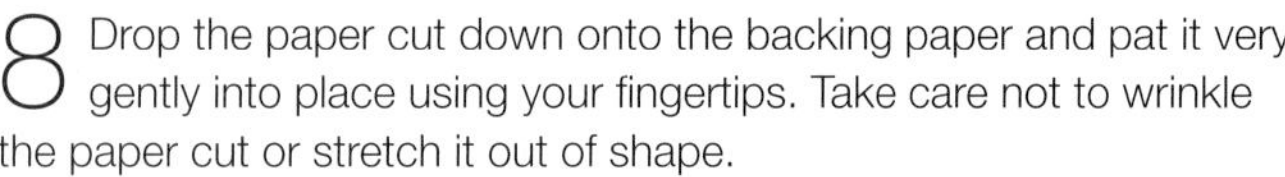

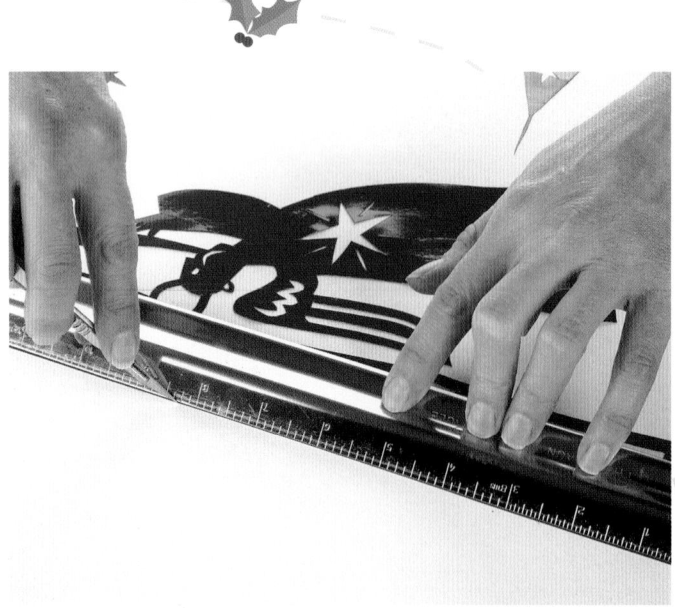

10 When the glue is dry, trim away the excess white paper with a craft knife and metal ruler.

Hint **Rubber rollers are used when printing from linocuts and are available from specialist stores. If you can't get hold of one, simply press down firmly with your thumbs, working from the centre of each element out towards the edges.**

Christmas Coasters

If you feel daunted by the idea of making a large-scale paper cut like the table runner, trace off the images you like and use them to produce coasters instead. You'll still have some Scandinavian Christmas style, but in a fraction of the time.

Fairy Jewellery Box

Perfect for a young girl, this decorative box is ideal for presenting a piece of jewellery or another small item such as a fine scarf or diary. Its paper cuts are relatively simple, so the only challenge is in placing the different cut outs to create a balanced effect. As with all the designs in this book, feel free to change the colours used to suit a particular room scheme.

This design was inspired by the technique of silhouette paper cutting, in which black paper portraits of people in profile were pasted onto white paper backgrounds. This was a very popular pastime in the 19th century, and was widely practiced in Europe and the United States, mainly by young ladies.

The design uses three different papers plus the cream of the painted box to create a sense of depth.

To emphasize that this is a jewellery box, the fairies around the edge are holding a ring. You could highlight this element – or any other – with an overlay of gold paper. If this isn't going to be a jewellery box, put a heart in place of the ring.

Recalling the beautiful fairy paintings of the 1920s and 1930s, like those by Arthur Rackham, who famously illustrated the first edition of Peter Pan and other stories, this lovely design is ideal for any little girl who dreams of being a fairy princess.

Fairy Jewellery Box

you will need

- 18cm (7in) diameter round cardboard box with lid
- A4 sheet of dark and light lilac paper
- A4 sheet of aqua paper
- Cream emulsion paint
- Decorator's paintbrush and artist's brush
- Small coin
- Water-based acrylic varnish
- Basic tool kit

Inspiration

This design fits on a 18cm (7in) diameter box, but you can scale it up or down using a photocopier to fit a larger or smaller box.

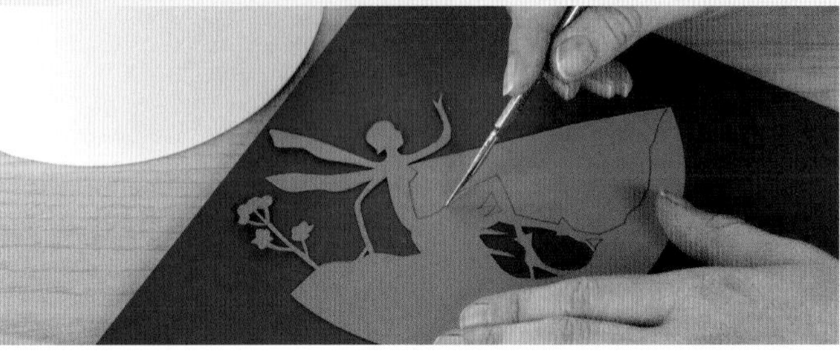

1 Paint the box with two coats of cream emulsion paint. For the box lid, trace the fairy template from page 113 and transfer it to light lilac paper. Cut out the design using a craft knife on a cutting mat.

2 Trace the flowers and transfer these to aqua paper. As before, cut out the design using a craft knife.

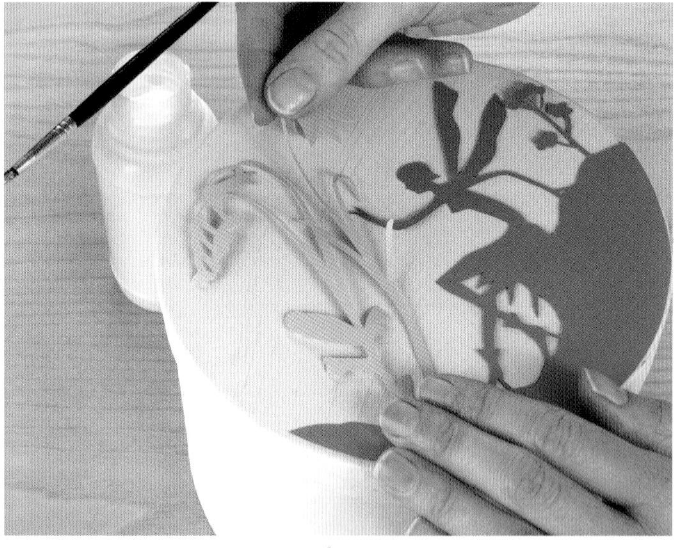

3 Flip both the paper cuts so the pencil lines are on the reverse. Use PVA glue applied with a small brush to stick the fairy to the top of the box lid, matching the curve.

4 Glue the flowers to the top of the box lid, positioning them around the fairy's arm, as shown here.

Hint To make sure that you place the coin in the same way each time, first draw a line across the coin using a ruler and permanent marker. Then place the coin on the paper so that the line runs exactly along the edge.

5 Cut a thin strip of aqua paper to fit around the side of the lid. Cut a second strip to the same length from the dark lilac paper. Draw semicircles along the lilac strip using a small coin as a template. Cut out to make a scalloped edge.

6 Glue the strip of aqua paper around the lid then glue the scalloped lilac strip on top, as shown.

7 Cut a 1.5cm (½in) wide strip of dark lilac paper and glue it around the base of the box. Trace and transfer the smaller fairies and stars to pale lilac and aqua paper. Cut them out and glue them around the sides of the box, starting with the fairies and spacing them as evenly as possible.

8 When the glue is dry, seal the box and lid with two coats of water-based acrylic varnish, leaving it to dry between coats.

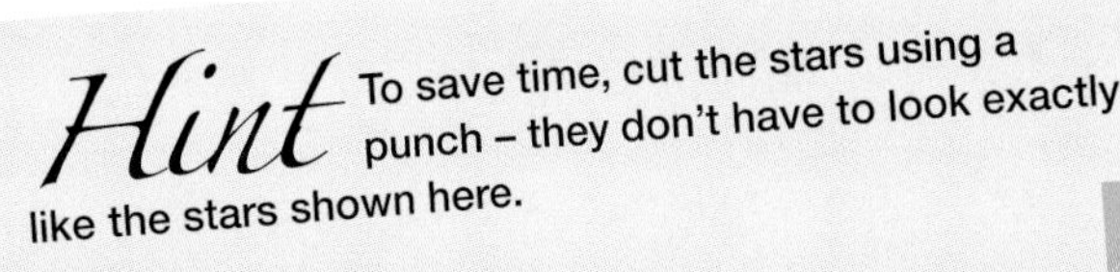
Hint To save time, cut the stars using a punch – they don't have to look exactly like the stars shown here.

Scoring and Folding

Scoring and folding, also known as paper sculpture, is the art of transforming the flat surface of two-dimensional paper into three dimensions. This is achieved by rolling and curving the paper and by scoring shallow lines into the surface so that it can be folded, bent and pinched into a sculptural form. This is easy and basic designs cut from flat paper can be transformed in exciting ways using only a few simple cuts and score lines. The light bounces off the different planes, creating shadows that dramatically mould the paper into sculptural forms.

Paper sculpture has been widely used in commercial settings – it was very popular for use in window displays in the US and Europe, especially after the Second World War. It is also a very important art form as wonderfully detailed paper sculptures can be produced.

MATERIALS

Choosing colour
Your choice of paper is probably the most important aspect of the technique. Some purists will only use white paper, and rely on light to sculpt their work with light and dark shadows. This can have stunning results, so white paper may be your ultimate choice. Handmade Indian and Nepalese paper is also good, because it comes in spectacular colours and designs. Choose the kind that has a hard, flat surface. The softer, bulkier types are too saggy. When choosing card, make sure that it is coloured on front and back and that the colour runs all the way through.

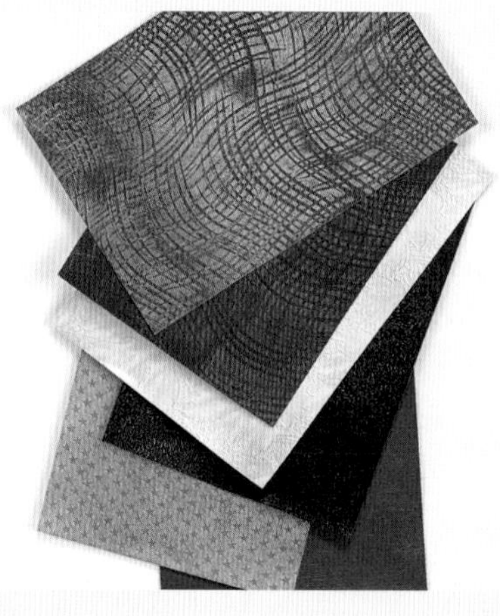

Perfect paper weight
I find the paper that gives the best results for most items is medium to heavy-weight artists' watercolour paper. This comes in all sizes up to A1 and has a slightly raised surface. It is easy to work with and gives great results because it folds crisply and is easy to score without making ragged edges. For larger items, I use medium-weight card or a combination of light and medium-weight. The thicker card is heavy enough to stay rigid when cut and folded and so is good for basic structures. Detail can be added afterwards with thinner card that is easier to score.

TECHNIQUES

Making a straight score
To score on a straight line, run the back of a craft knife against the edge of a metal ruler, as shown. Remember that your paper will bend away, or outwards, from the cut surface of the score line, so you must make sure you score on the correct side. Bend the paper gently along the score line.

Making a curved score
A curved score line can be done by eye if you are feeling confident, or you can lightly trace the score line first in pencil. Score with the back of a craft knife as for a straight score. Once the paper is scored, squeeze it gently between your fingers and thumbs to widen the split and shape the paper.

Lavender-scented Card

Based on traditional pomander designs, this simple raised heart is the perfect introduction to scoring and folding paper. The exciting principle of adding form and dimension to a flat paper shape is very clearly demonstrated with two simple cuts and some basic scoring. Making a shape three-dimensional also adds function, in this case to create a container for lavender on a lovely Mother's Day card.

you will need

- A4 sheet of gingham paper
- A4 sheet of medium-weight lilac card
- Scraps of medium-weight purple paper
- Eyelet punch and hammer
- Scallop-edge scissors
- Dried lavender
- Basic tool kit

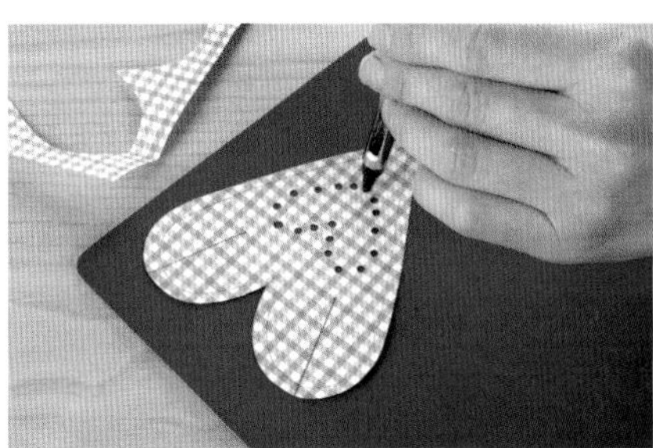

1 Trace and transfer the large heart from page 106 onto gingham paper and cut it out. Place the heart on a cutting mat and punch evenly spaced holes into the paper in a heart shape to allow the lavender scent to filter through.

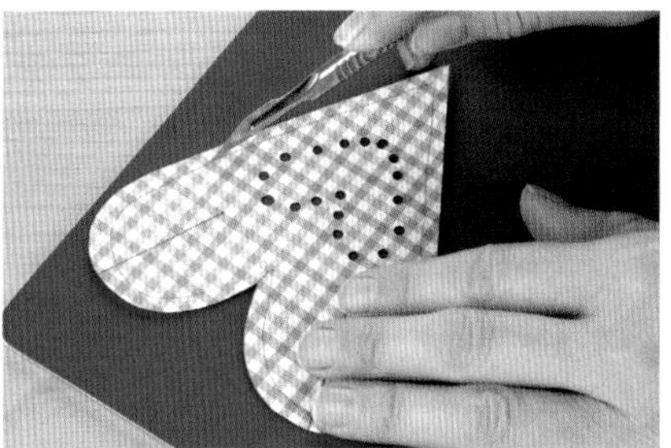

2 On the back of the heart, score a border 5mm (¼in) in from the edge of the heart, where marked. Use a ruler and craft knife to make the two diagonal cuts in the left and right side of the heart where marked on the template.

Hint Dried lavender, like all dried herbs, loses its scent over time, so buy it in small quantities as you need it. Store any leftover lavender in a sealed lightproof bag or tin to maximize its lifespan.

3 Overlap the tops of the heart at the cut by about 1.5cm (¾in) and glue the flaps together. Trim away the excess paper to give a smooth curve. Snip the border around the heart every 1cm (½in), cutting as far as the score line. Fold up the border (see step 4).

4 Fold a 29 x 15cm (11½ x 6in) rectangle of lilac card in half to make the greetings card. Glue one side of the heart to the front, pour in a handful of dried lavender and glue down the other side. Cut a thin strip of purple paper with scallop-edge scissors and glue it around the heart, trimming to fit as necessary.

Summer Lanterns

These versatile lanterns, inspired by lanterns and lampshades from Japan and China, can be hung from a pagoda for a summer party, used as indoor decorations or made on a much smaller scale and strung together in garlands to decorate a child's bedroom. They're not intended for use as lampshades with light bulbs, and shouldn't be used as such. Each lantern is made in the same way, but the cylinders of paper are cut and scored differently, varying the width of the strips to expand and contract the paper. The incredible variety of form and structure achievable simply by cutting and scoring the surface of a paper cylinder is such fun that you'll want to experiment yourself.

Made from fairly thick handmade paper, this lantern holds it shape even once cut. The blue paper shade is enhanced with simple borders at top and bottom and hung from a wire loop.

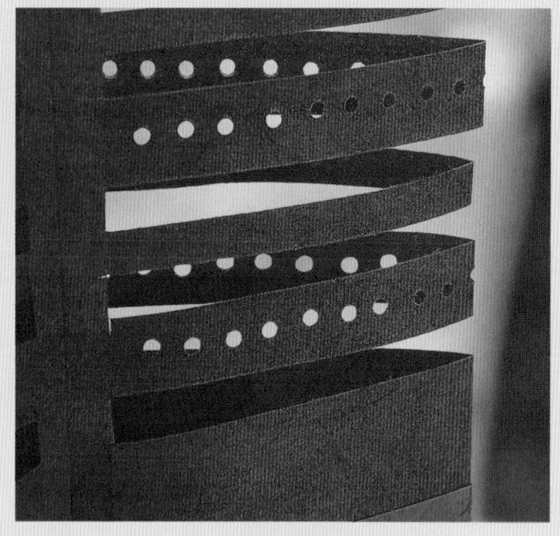

Pushing in alternate tabs at the corners creates a stepped effect rather like that of a skyscraper.

These brightly coloured lanterns make wonderful party decorations and help to set a joyful, frivolous mood. Instructions are provided for making the blue lantern, and there are many other simple variations you could try.

Summer Lanterns

you will need

- A2 sheet of decorative blue handmade paper
- A4 sheets of pink and green handmade paper
- Zigzag scissors
- Florists' stump wire
- Flat-head pliers
- Coordinating ribbon from which to hang the lantern
- Basic tool kit

Hint Read through all the instructions and look at the step-by-step photographs carefully before you score and cut the decorative tabs to make sure you cut in the right place.

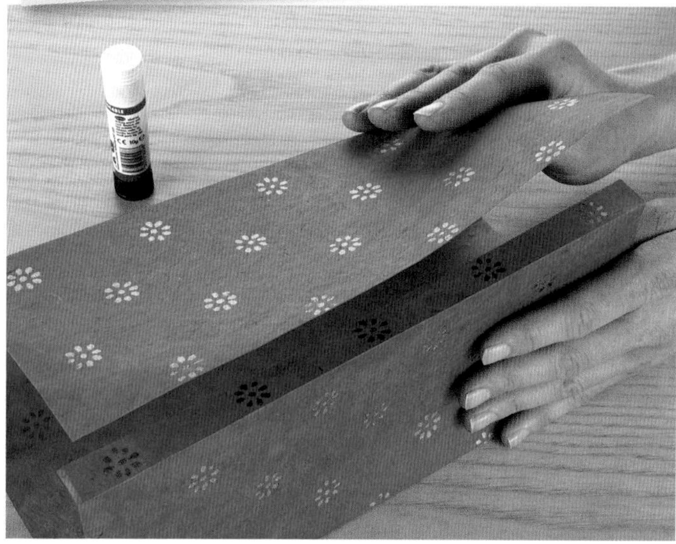

1 Cut a 45 x 28cm (17½ x 11in) rectangle of decorative blue paper. On the front of the paper, lightly score a line every 11cm (4¼in) to divide it into four panels (see page 74). The last score line will leave a narrow border 1cm (½in) wide.

2 Gently fold the paper along the score lines. Fold under the border and glue it under the opposite side to create the cuboid shape of the lantern. Flatten the lantern in half.

3 Very lightly draw a vertical line 3cm (1in) to the right of each fold, as shown. Starting 2cm (¾in) down from the top of the lantern, mark lines 1cm (½in) apart, from each pencil line across to each fold. Stop 2cm (¾in) above the lower edge of the lantern.

4 Keeping the paper folded, cut along the pencil lines with scissors to make tabs. Repeat at each fold.

Inspiration

Experiment with other materials. A lantern made from coloured foil could look wonderful or you could try using coloured acetate.

5 Flatten each corner then very lightly score the sides of every other tab on both sides of the fold, starting at the top.

6 Cut two 2cm (¾in) wide strips of pink paper with zigzag scissors. Glue a strip around the top and bottom edges of the lantern. Cut two thin strips of green paper and glue these along the centres of the pink borders.

7 Once the borders are dry, fold each corner again. Starting at the top of the lantern, push alternate tabs inwards towards the centre of the lantern to make a step pattern.

8 To make a hanger, cut an 18cm (7in) length of florists' wire. Wrap the middle of the wire around a pencil and twist to make a loop. Pierce a hole at two opposite corners of the top of the lantern. Poke the ends of the wires through the holes and curl up the very ends with a pair of pliers. Tie a length of ribbon from the centre of the hanger to suspend the lantern.

Easter Chicken Basket

Make this quirky Easter chicken to contain some tasty springtime treats, such as tiny foil-wrapped chocolate eggs, and learn some basic sculpting techniques in the process. Shaping the paper creates a three-dimensional effect, while punched holes add texture and allow light to pass through. The techniques are simple and the end result utterly charming.

This chicken is made from sugar paper, which is designed for use with soft pastels because the texture holds the chalky colours in place. You can buy it from art shops in large sheets or books of mixed colours. Don't worry if you can't find the exact colours used here – chickens come in all shapes, colours and sizes and so can your chicken basket.

Punched holes on the wings and tail provide an additional decorative element and create a lovely lacy look.

The pink dots on the chicken's body, made from punched shapes, help to coordinate the colours of the chicken.

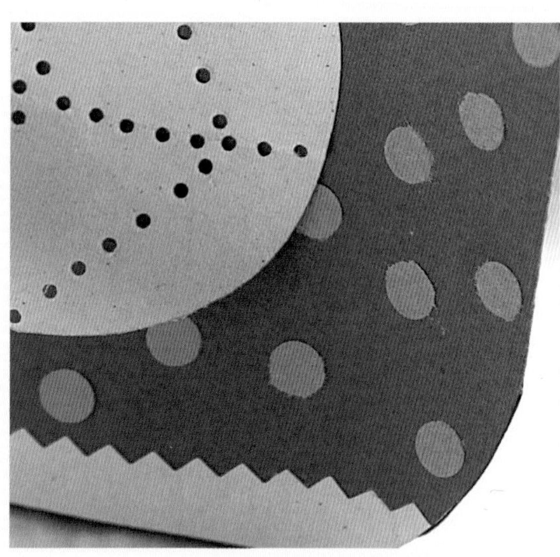

What a wonderful gift – a handmade container stuffed with Easter goodies that anyone would be delighted to receive. The shaped paper pieces and punched holes call to mind American tinware designs and as such create an Old World feel.

Easter Chicken Basket

you will need

- Chocolate brown sugar paper: one 36 x 17cm (14¼ x 6¾in) rectangle and one 12.5 x 10cm (5 x 4in) rectangle
- Dusty pink sugar paper: an A4 sheet is plenty
- Yellow sugar paper: an A4 sheet is plenty
- Scoring or embossing tool (or use the back of your knife)
- Zigzag scissors or pinking shears
- Hole punch
- Eyelet punch and hammer
- Basic tool kit

Hint Read through all the instructions before you begin. You'll find it saves time in the long run if you have an overview of the entire project as you work each stage.

1 Trace all the hen pattern pieces from page 116 and transfer them to thin white card. Cut out the shapes to make templates. Fold the large rectangle of brown paper in half. Position the hen's body template on the paper, with the neck along the fold. Draw round the template and then cut out the shape.

2 Open out the hen's body. Replace the template and draw around the beak onto the back of the head. Working on a cutting mat and using a craft knife, cut along the top and bottom of the beak only. Cut a 1.5cm (½in) slit down the fold of the neck, starting from the base of the beak. Now trace the beak and transfer the shape to yellow sugar paper. Cut out the yellow beak.

3 Transfer and cut out the rest of the hen from appropriately coloured paper. Score the front of the hen's comb where indicated on the pattern. Crease along the score lines to make it three-dimensional. Glue the comb in place on the back of the hen's head and glue the wattle in the slit on the hen's neck, folding the card in half before the glue sets to check the positioning (see step 4).

Inspiration

Pad the inside of the finished chicken with straw then top with mini chocolate eggs as a delightful Easter present. Other small items would also work well – tiny toy chicks, little Easter cakes or Easter biscuit, for example.

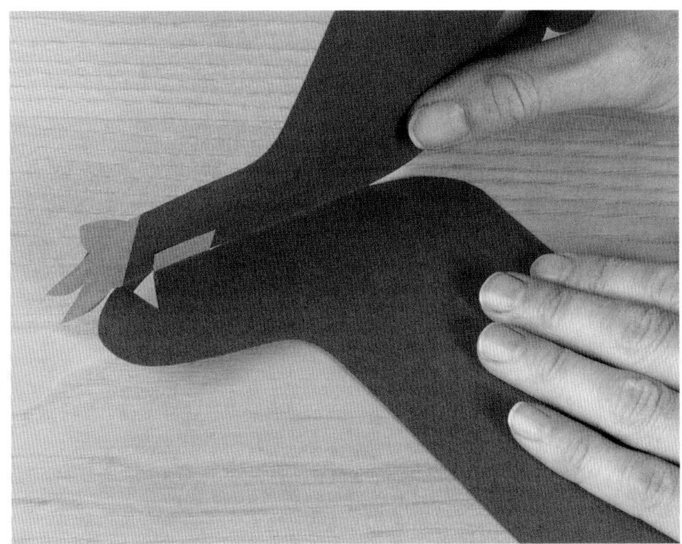

4 Push out the hen's beak then fold the body together and glue just the neck section. Glue the yellow beak in place. To make the eye, punch a circle from yellow paper. Make a hole in the centre with an eyelet punch. Glue in place on the hen.

5 Curve the hen's body round to make a circle, and glue the edges together at the back. Cut two 1 x 29cm (⅜ x 11½in) strips of yellow paper with pinking shears. Glue in place at the neck and along the lower edge of the hen's body. Punch pink dots using the hole punch and glue them randomly over the hen's body.

6 Score the feathers and wings where indicated on the pattern. Fold all the pieces carefully along the score lines to make them three-dimensional. Use an eyelet punch and hammer to make lines of decorative holes around the tops and bottoms of the feathers and along the wings, using the photograph on page 79 as your guide.

7 Fold and glue the bases of the feathers together. Glue them around the back of the hen, varying their heights. Glue the top halves of the wings to the sides of the hen to finish.

Gingerbread House

With its glitter-frosted roof, shuttered windows and bronze polka-dot walls, this fabulous gingerbread house makes a wonderful table decoration for the festive season. And as if that wasn't enough, it has a hidden twist – the windows, doors and trees have little flaps that open to make an advent calendar that can be used year after year.

The house may look complicated, but the basic construction is simple; it just requires careful scoring and folding before assembly. The main walls are joined with scored tabs and the roof is hinged at the top. The windows, doors, trees and even the roof are all completed before being stuck in place so you can work in easy stages.

The use of metallic and glitter card plus glitter glue and glitter dust capture the sparkle of frost on this lovely gingerbread house.

Each flap has a number on the front so that it can be opened on the appropriate day. These were printed onto tracing paper from a computer and added randomly in the traditional manner. If you prefer, you can use number stickers or write the number on a plain round sticker using a permanent marker pen.

This superb gingerbread house will delight all who see it. Almost good enough to eat, it makes the perfect centrepiece for a winter tea party.

8
16
19
21
24
12

Gingerbread House

you will need

- 10 sheets of A4 medium weight bronze card (or one A1 sheet)
- A4 sheet of white glitter card
- Green metallic card
- Metallic paper in different colours for the punched dots and end wall decorations
- Shiny festive stickers including stars
- Translucent glitter glue
- White glitter dust
- Bradawl
- Paintbrush
- Hole punch
- Snowflake punch
- Scallop-edge and zigzag scissors or pinking shears
- Silver cake board
- Basic tool kit

1 Trace the house walls, end and roof panels from page 117 onto bronze-coloured card. Cut out all the pieces. On the front of the card, score along the lines where marked on the patterns.

2 To make the diamond patterns on the walls, measure and mark the positions of evenly spaced criss-cross lines. Lightly score the lines then dot across them with a bradawl.

3 Punch circles from metallic paper and glue them to the house walls between the scored lines. Lightly brush over the walls with glitter glue to make them extra sparkly.

4 Trace, transfer and cut out 20 rows of roof tiles from bronze card. Trace a snowflake onto each tile where marked and along the tiles at the base of each side of the roof. Prick out the shapes of the snowflakes with a bradawl.

5 Squeeze a line of glitter glue around the tiles. Before the glue dries, sprinkle glitter dust onto the tiles, then pour the excess glitter back into the jar and leave the tiles to dry.

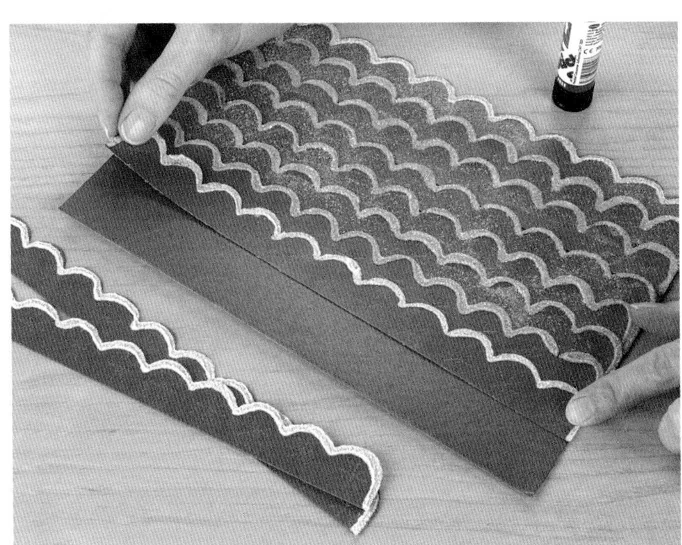

6 Glue 10 strips of tiles to each roof panel, overlapping them slightly. Lightly brush over the tiles with glitter glue to make them extra sparkly.

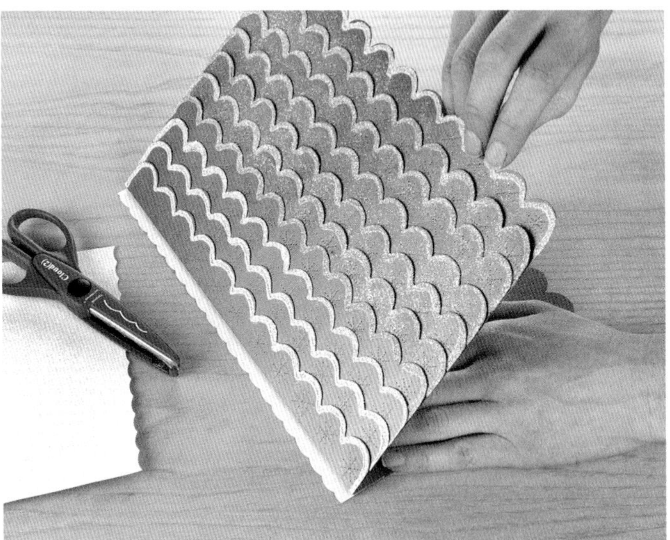

7 Cut a 1.5cm (½in) wide strip of white glitter card to fit along the top of the roof using scallop-edge scissors. Sandwich the glitter strip between the two halves of the roof and glue it in place. Glue more strips to the side edges of the roof.

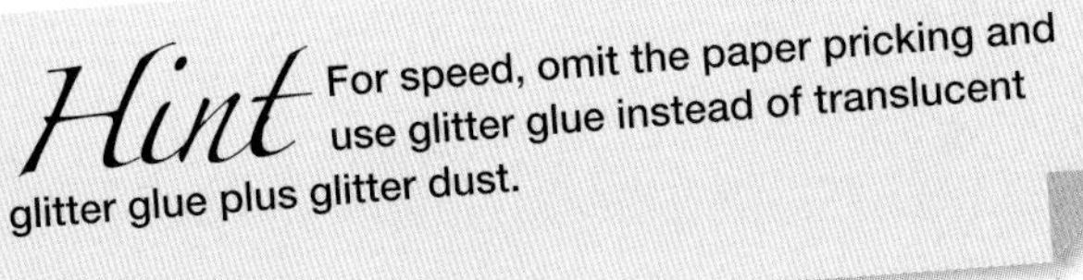

Hint For speed, omit the paper pricking and use glitter glue instead of translucent glitter glue plus glitter dust.

Inspiration

Behind each flap is some coloured metallic paper decorated with a contrasting festive sticker. You could replace these with small photographs of family members or other stickers. You could even attach a tiny tag that a child could exchange for a small sweet or toy.

8 Cut 1cm (⅜in) wide strips of metallic paper to fit across the upper half of the front and back walls. Cut a decorative edge along one side of each strip with zigzag scissors. Glue in place with the zigzag edge at the bottom and trim away the excess paper.

9 Carefully fold over the wall flaps along the scored lines. Glue the walls together to form the house. Glue the house to an A4 sheet of bronze card to make the base then trim away the excess card.

10 Trace and transfer the doors, windows and heart from page 117 onto bronze card. Cut open the windows where marked. Glue metallic paper to fit the backs of all the pieces so it shows through the windows and decorate with festive stickers (or see Inspiration above).

11 Decorate all the pieces with glitter glue. Sprinkle with glitter dust, then pour off the excess and leave to dry. Punch out some snowflakes from white glitter card and glue one at the top of each window. Print out the numbers 1 to 24 onto tracing paper. Cut out the numbers and glue them randomly to all the advent windows.

12 Trace four Christmas trees from page 117 onto white glitter card and cut them out. Decorate with dots of metallic paper. Glue the windows and doors to the front and back walls then glue the trees to these walls too.

13 Glue the remaining doors and windows around the side walls, using the photographs here and on page 83 as your guide.

14 Spread a line of PVA glue along the flaps on the side walls. Lower the roof onto the house, pressing it gently onto the wall flaps. Leave to dry thoroughly.

15 Place the house on a silver cake board. Trace and transfer the tree from page 117 to green card and cut out. Decorate with punched shapes and attach to the side of the board. Cut a 2cm (¾in) wide strip of green metallic paper with zigzag scissors and tape it around the base of the board to make grass.

Fabulous Feathering

Feathering is paper fringing, created by snipping at regular intervals along one edge. It adds bulk and dimension, and is great for representing natural materials such as grass and foliage. The cuts may be broad or narrow, and the narrower they are, the more the paper will flick upwards. As an extra refinement, lightweight paper may be curled manually by rolling the fringes tightly around a pencil, or pulling the fringes over the blades of a pair of scissors to produce the same effect.

Paper feathering is found in the paper crafts of many countries, especially Mexico, where large-scale masks and puppets are created for fiestas, religious festivals and carnival parades. Hollow papier-mâché figures, called piñatas, are traditionally made for children in Mexico, and they are often covered with layer upon layer of fringed tissue-paper strips.

TOOLS AND TECHNIQUES

Different papers, different effects
A hard, smooth paper like vellum will produce very clean, precise feathering, and if the cuts are made close together, the paper will curl up dramatically, like eyelashes. Crepe paper has the extra dimension of stretchiness, and will produce shaggy fronds that are very eye catching and dramatic. For a very curly effect, choose a lightweight (80–120gsm) paper. If you simply want to roll the paper into curves, medium- to heavy-weight paper is very effective while if you want flat feathering, with no extra curling, then tissue paper is excellent.

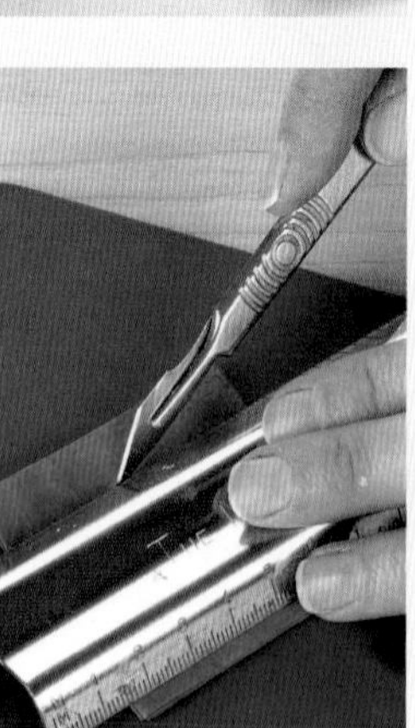

Scoring first
To ensure even fringing, create a scored guide line to show how far the cuts should go. First fold the paper several times. Now score a line a short distance from one long edge using the back of your craft knife or an embossing tool.

Cutting the feathers
Snip the paper at regular intervals up to the scored line. You can do this by eye or mark where to cut along the lower edge before you start using a ruler and pencil.

Curling the feathers
With medium-weight paper, gently pull the closed blades of a pair of scissors down the fringing, as shown. Tissue paper can be rolled gently around a pencil and heavy-weight paper may also need this treatment because it is so thick. You may need to hold the paper around the pencil for several seconds to help it keep its shape.

Lavish Lion Card

A cheerful lion stalks across this highly tactile child's card. Its mane and tail are made from feathered medium-weight brown paper, which stands out boldly in contrast to the feathery palm leaves above it that are finely fringed and seem to flicker in the light like real leaves. Below the lion is the lush green grass of the African plain, which is long and curled, bowed down under a hot sun. You'll love making this card and it's a great opportunity to try out a range of fabulous feathering techniques.

you will need

- 35 x 25cm (14 x 10in) rectangle of medium-weight turquoise card folded in half to make a 17.5 x 25cm (7 x 10in) card
- A4 sheets of sand and dark brown paper
- A4 sheet of lime green paper
- Scraps of yellow, orange, red and dark green paper
- Basic tool kit

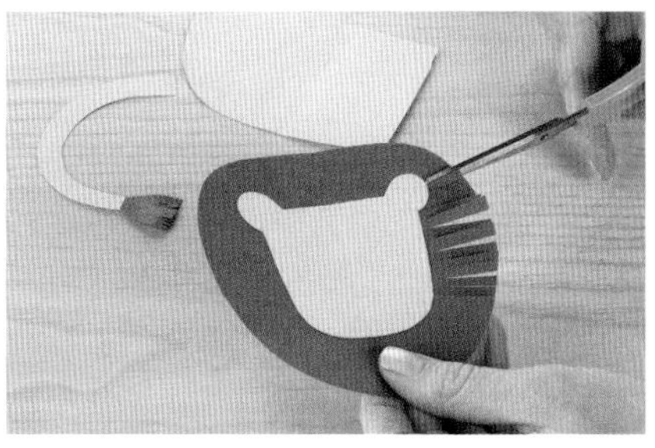

1 Trace the lion pieces from page 118. Transfer the pieces to appropriate coloured paper and cut out. Glue the head to the mane and the tail end to the tail; leave to dry. Now snip all the way around the mane, up to the edge of the lion's head.

2 Gently pull the strands of the lion's mane over the closed blades of a pair of scissors to curve the paper upwards slightly. Snip the tail and curve the paper in the same way. Stick the eyes, nose and mouth on the lion's face.

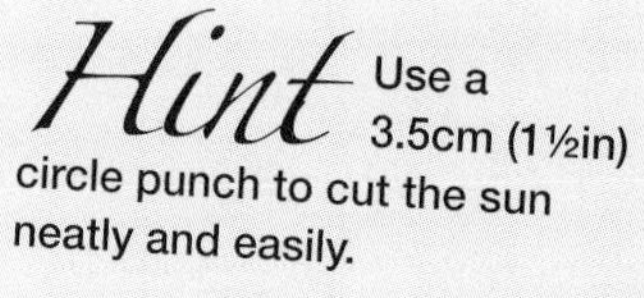

3 Cut an 8cm x 17.5cm (3 x 7in) wide strip of green paper. Feather one edge, curling the feathers over scissors as explained left. Glue the lion to the turquoise card. Glue the grass on top.

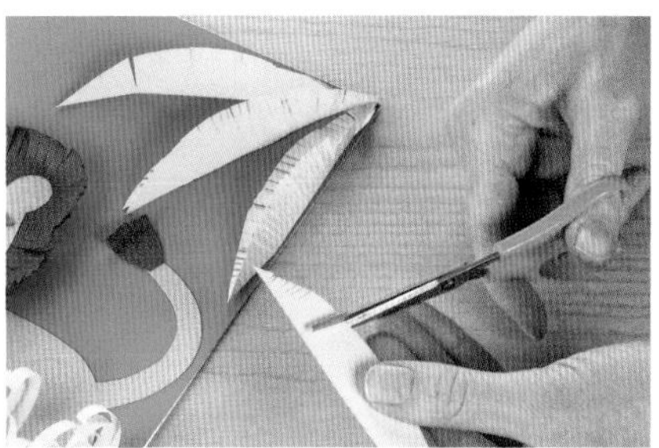

4 Trace four palm leaves from page 119 and cut them from green paper. Fold the leaves in half then snip along the edges. Glue the leaves in position. Cut a sun from yellow paper and glue in place.

Floral Wreath

This delicate feathered paper wreath is perfect for a spring wedding or a celebration such as Mother's Day or Easter. Mount it on a wall or door hung from some organza ribbon or omit the ribbon and make a smaller version to place around a candle as a centrepiece. The flowers are in the spring colours of yellow and purple but you can choose whatever colours you like.

The wreath is based on a circlet of coiled wire, which is wrapped in feathered white crepe paper for an organic, bushy effect. Overlapping the paper strips forces out the fringes, so they have much more volume, completely hiding the wire beneath. The flowers also have fringed paper centres for body and to coordinate the effect.

This lovely paper wreath can be hung on a wall or door, worn as a headdress by a bridesmaid or carried in place of flowers and will be a lasting memento of a wonderful occasion.

The centre of each flower is a tightly rolled strip of fringed yellow tissue paper, which has been fanned out into a pompom shape. Once you've made the flower centres, it's a relatively simple matter to glue the petals and leaves around it.

This gorgeous wreath not only looks good but it is surprisingly quick to make. It looks lovely hung on the wall for a celebration, but it would also make a wonderful decoration for a little girl's room.

Floral Wreath

you will need

- Pack of white crepe paper
- Scraps of yellow, green and purple tissue paper
- Coiled wire
- Wire cutters
- 2.5cm (1in) wide white organza ribbon, as long as you like
- Basic tool kit

Hint The leaves and petals don't have to be made with crepe paper – you could use any lightweight paper you have in your cupboards, including vellum.

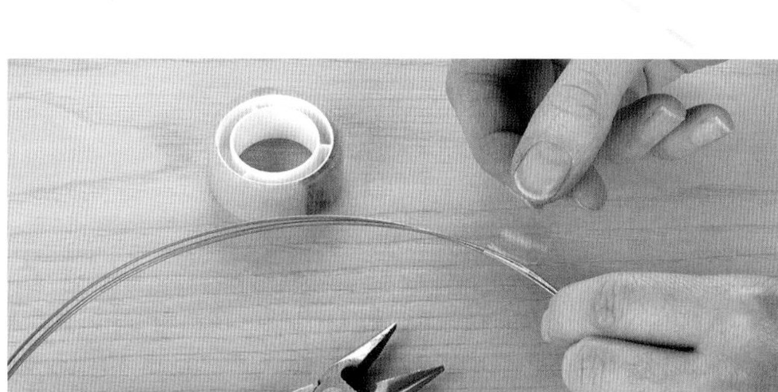

1 To make the frame for the wreath, cut three coils of wire with pliers. Form into a circle approximately 20cm (8in) in diameter. Tape the wire at top and bottom to keep the coils together.

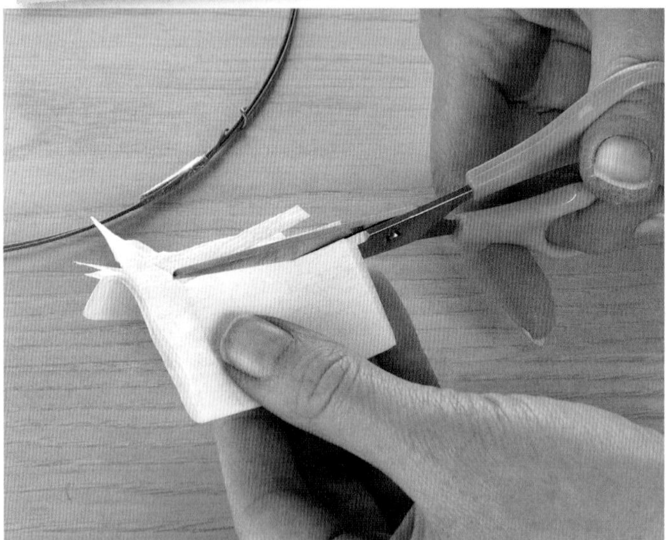

2 Cut a 120cm (47in) length of white crepe paper 6cm (2½in) wide. Fold it several times so it measures about 6cm (2½in) long. Score a line 1cm (½in) down from the top edge then snip along the length, making cuts as far as the scored line.

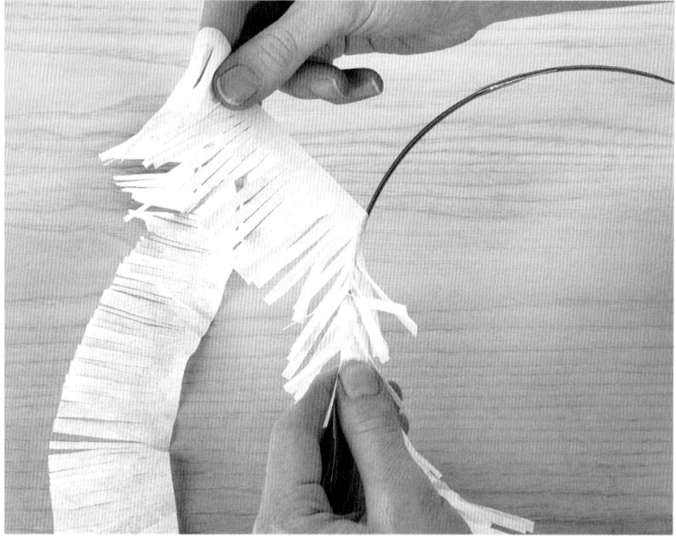

3 Unfold the paper, and tape one end to the wire. Wrap it around and around the wire circle. Overlap the paper slightly so all the wire is covered. Tape the free end of the paper to the wire.

Inspiration

A simple wreath like this is very easy to adapt for different occasions. For example, replacing the flowers with blown quail eggs would make a lovely Easter wreath, while silver, gold and metallic papers could be used for Christmas.

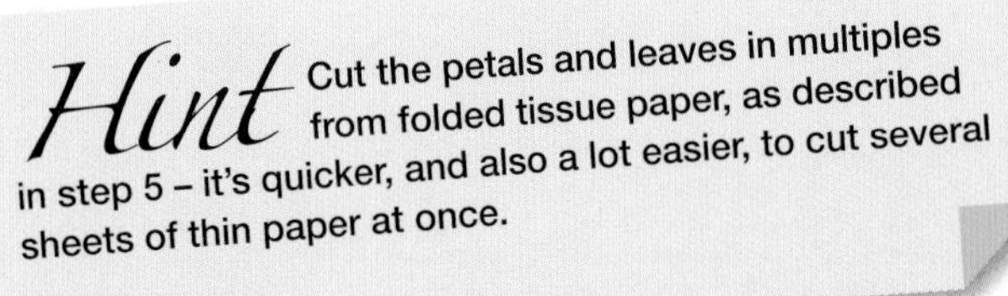

Hint **Cut the petals and leaves in multiples from folded tissue paper, as described in step 5 – it's quicker, and also a lot easier, to cut several sheets of thin paper at once.**

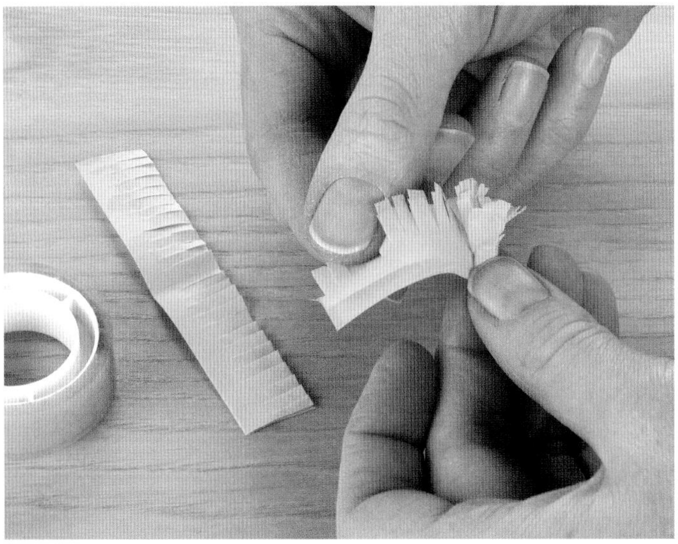

4 To make the flower centres, cut 1.5cm (½in) wide strips of yellow tissue paper. Fold over each one several times then feather it as before. Unfold the paper and roll it up tightly; tape the end in place so that it doesn't unravel. Fan out the fringing to fluff it up a little. You'll need eight flower centres.

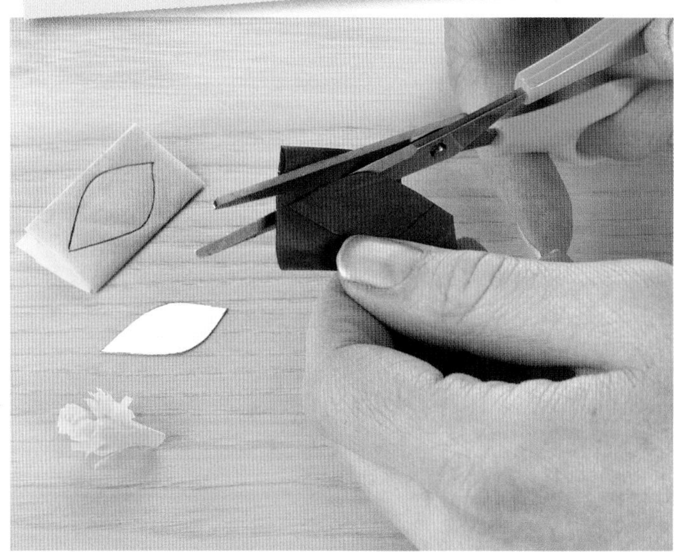

5 Trace the petal and leaf pattern from page 119 and transfer it to thin white card to make a template. For each flower, fold a piece of purple tissue paper and a piece of green tissue paper into four. Draw around the template onto the paper and cut out to make purple petals and green leaves.

6 Take the purple petals and glue them around the yellow flower centres, spacing them evenly at the top, bottom and sides. Add the green leaves in the same way, placing them between the petals. Make a total of eight flowers.

7 Glue the flowers to the wreath, spacing them evenly. Tie a length of white organza ribbon around one end of the wreath. You can either knot the ribbon in place and use it for hanging or tie a generous ribbon bow and leave long tails to hang down.

Fringed Envelope Bag

Designed to hold a birthday invitation, this elegant envelope bag is decorated with bands of frothy vellum feathering for a luxurious and frivolous effect. The bag is finished with another example of feathering, a gold vellum tassel. This is simple to make by tightly rolling a strip of feathered paper.

Vellum used to be quite hard to come by except in a very limited range, but as paper crafters have come to love its delicate qualities, more and more types have become available. You can buy it from art suppliers, craft stores and from scrapbooking specialists.

They say that presentation is everything, and this fine envelope certainly fits the bill.

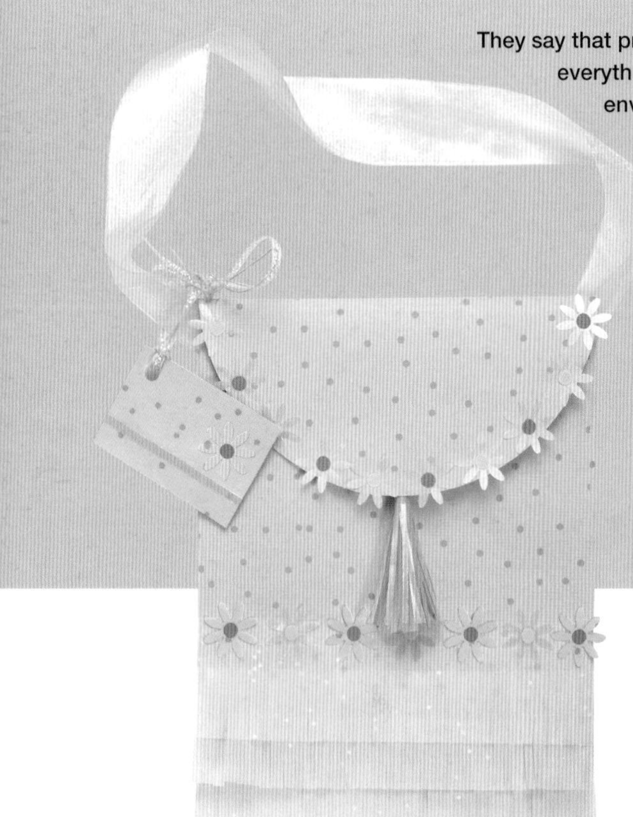

This pretty tag was made from a 15 x 5cm (6 x 2in) strip of blue dotty paper folded in half. A punched daisy and strip of gold paper add simple but stylish embellishment to the front.

This envelope bag is so gorgeous that it is a present in itself. It is perfect for presenting gift vouchers or a child's artwork, or you could create a mini scrapbook page, perhaps including a lock of a child's hair, confetti or other memorabilia.

Fringed Envelope Bag

you will need

- Large sheet of dotty pink paper
- A4 sheet of white sparkly vellum
- A4 sheet of pale gold vellum
- Dotty blue paper for the daisies: an A4 sheet is ample
- Pink paper for the daisies: an A4 sheet is ample
- Double-sided tape
- Daisy punch
- Hole punch
- 50cm (20in) length of pink organza ribbon
- Basic tool kit

Inspiration

Consider the colours and designs of the card you intend to present in this lovely envelope before you begin. It's a nice idea to choose colours and themes for the envelope that reflect those of the card within.

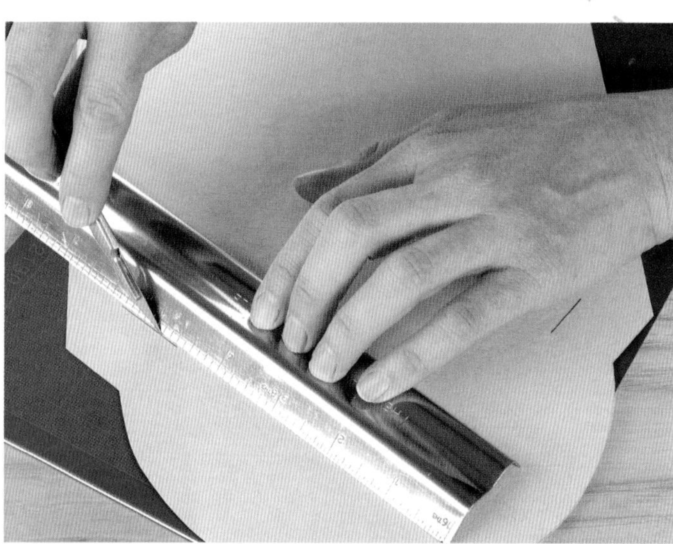

1 Trace the bag template from page 119 and transfer it to the paper in pencil. Cut out the bag using scissors or a knife. Now cut two slits with a craft knife on the upper part of the bag where marked on the pattern for the ribbon handles.

Hint Before you start cutting up your best paper, make a test envelope bag from scrap paper up to step 3 so you understand how it is constructed. This ensures you won't make any expensive errors. You can also use your test envelope to help adapt the pattern to fit specific cards.

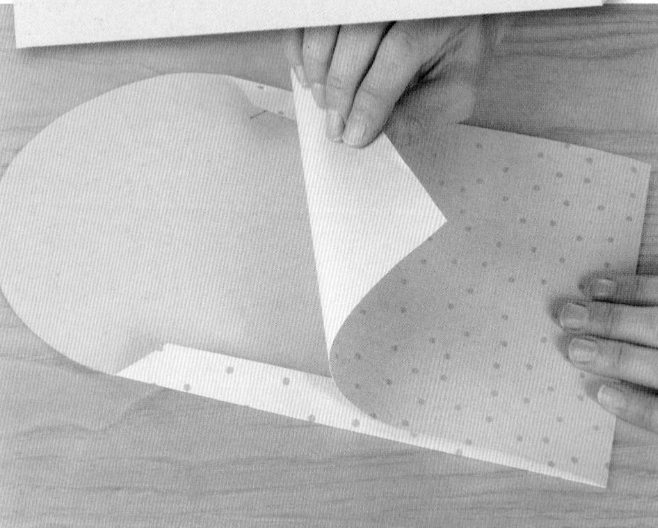

2 Score and fold in the side flaps on the top of the bag level with the lower part of the bag as indicated on the pattern. Fold up the lower section of the bag and glue it over the sides. Fold down the curved flap where marked.

3 Cut four 5cm (2in) deep strips of white sparkly vellum to fit across the bag. Score a horizontal line along each strip, 1cm (⅜in) down from the top edge. Snip up from the lower edge to the scored line to create fringing, as shown.

Hint Vellum is ideal for feathering because it is can be cut very precisely and always gives a sharp, clean appearance.

4 Starting at the lower edge, attach a strip of fringed vellum to the bag with double-sided tape. Attach the remaining strips in the same way, overlapping them by about 2cm (¾in) each time.

5 Punch four blue and 13 pale gold daisies. Punch nine pink and eight blue flower centres using a hole punch. Glue blue and gold daisies along the top strip of fringing, alternating the colours. Glue gold daisies around the flap of the bag. Glue the flower centres in place, alternating the colours.

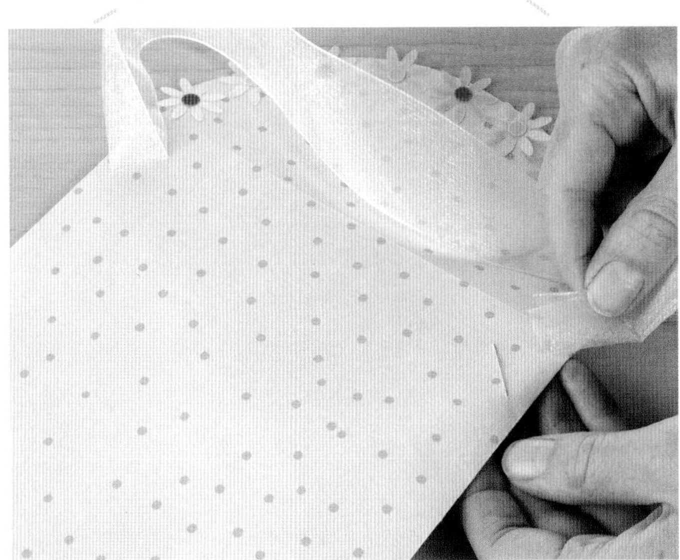

6 Thread each end of the pink organza ribbon through the slits at the top of the bag, from the outside to the inside. Secure the ends of the ribbon in place with double-sided tape.

7 Cut a 7 x 15cm (2¾ x 6in) strip of gold vellum. Snip along one edge. Roll up the strip to make a tassel, securing the top with double-sided tape. Attach the tassel to the front of the bag as a finishing touch.

Mini Christmas Tree

This final project, a table-top Christmas tree, combines my favourite technique, feathering, with my favourite material, crepe paper. It is constructed in much the same way as the wreath featured on page 90 by binding feathered paper around wire. You can have a lot of fun experimenting with the width of the feathering and the tightness of the overlapping.

The main inspirations for this little tree are goose-feather Christmas trees, which were first made in Germany over 100 years ago to help reduce the number of fir trees that were either cut down or lopped each year. They are made in a similar way to this little tree, by wrapping goose feathers around wire, but with wire branches fixed to a wooden dowel trunk.

The star decorations are cut from card and then covered with decorative paper. The gold and silver papers used here are very elegant, but you can use a selection of colours. If you want to save time, use double-sided holographic card or any other double-sided card that you think is suitable.

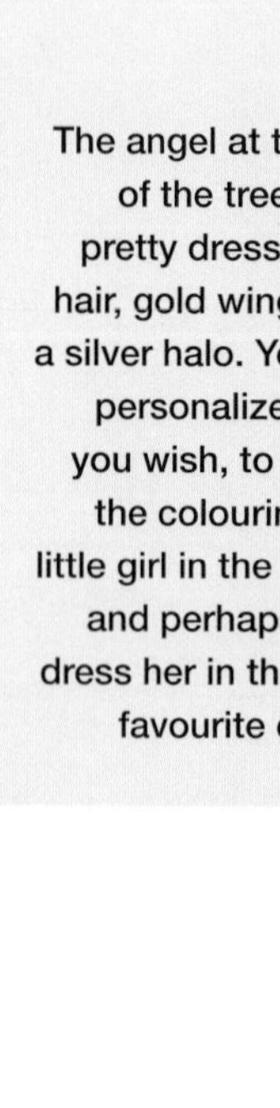

The angel at the top of the tree has a pretty dress, silver hair, gold wings and a silver halo. You can personalize her, if you wish, to match the colouring of a little girl in the family, and perhaps even dress her in the girl's favourite colour.

This magnificent tree is the perfect finale for this book. It's a large project but certainly achievable with a little care and attention. Personalize your tree and surround it with presents and it will have pride of place in your festivities every year.

Mini Christmas Tree

you will need

- Packet of green crepe paper
- Packet of red tissue paper
- A3 sheet of thin white card for stars
- Scraps of pink, gold, silver and decorative metallic papers for the angel and stars
- Silver doily for the angel's halo
- Strong wire
- Wire cutters
- Flat-nose pliers
- Small plant pot
- Brown modelling clay or Plasticine
- Hole punch
- Thin black pen to add the angel's features
- 28-gauge gold beading or similar wire to hang the stars
- Basic tool kit

Hint Different brands of crepe paper can vary greatly in strength and stretchiness. Try to find a thick, spongy variety for this project, because wrapping and overlapping really distorts and stretches it, making it much shaggier.

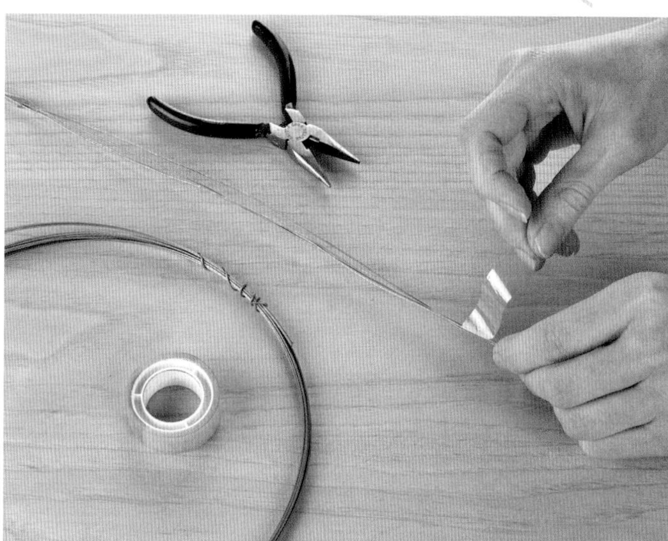

1 To make the tree trunk, cut a 184cm (72in) length of wire. Bend the wire in half, then in half again to make a length 46cm (18in) long. Tape the wire together to make a neat bundle.

2 To make the branches, cut 12 pieces of wire 13cm (5in) long and nine pieces 11.5cm (4½in) long. Bend each wire in half and tape the two ends together securely. Use flat-nose pliers to bend down the ends by 2cm (¾in).

3 To make the fringing, cut 21 strips of green crepe paper 25 x 4cm (10 x 1½in). Fold each strip of paper four times to make a short, thick wad, as shown.

Inspiration

This tree features traditional Christmas hues but you can use other colours. A stunning, multi-coloured effect can be achieved by wrapping two different-coloured strips of paper around the branches at the same time, and extra sparkle can be added with a touch of glitter dust.

4 Score each wad of paper 1cm (3⁄8in) in from the right-hand side. Snip the paper every 3mm (1⁄8in) along the opposite edge, as far as the score line, to fringe it.

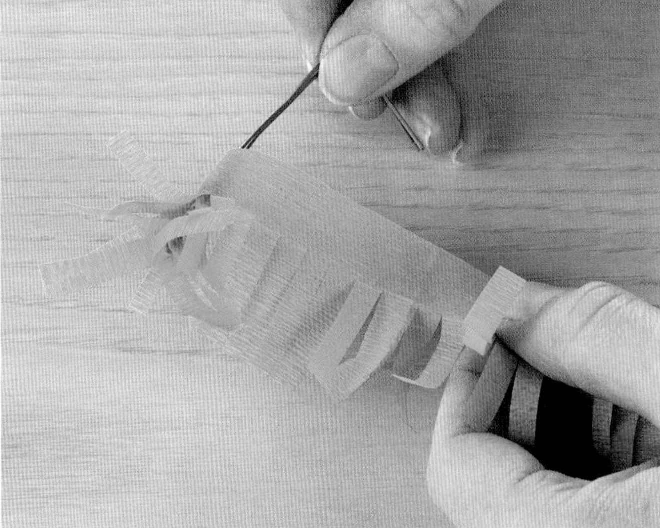

5 Unfold the fringed strips of paper. Take a strip of paper and tape one end to the straight end of a branch. Wrap the paper around the branch, overlapping the ends as you work. Keep the paper in place with a dab of paper glue when you reach the bend of the branch. Cut off the excess paper. Repeat to cover all the branches.

Hint An interesting technique is to stretch the edge of the strips widthways before you snip them. This will produce very curly feathering, and works best with wider strips of crepe paper.

6 Starting 5in (13cm) up from the end of the wire trunk, firmly tape the ends of six branches around the trunk at right angles to it. Try to space them fairly evenly round the truck but remember that because they are made of wire you can always shape them later.

7 Tape the next six branches in place 10cm (4in) above the first set. Tape five shorter branches 10cm (4in) above these, and the remaining four branches 8cm (3in) from the top of the tree. Now tape and wrap fringed paper around the trunk of the tree between the branches to cover the wire.

8 To make a firm base for the tree, fill a small plant pot with brown modelling clay or Plasticine.

9 Push the base of the tree trunk deep into the Plasticine, making sure it is straight.

Hint Give your tree some additional sparkle by using beads or florist's wired berries in place of the paper berries.

10 Cut 21 squares of red tissue paper 10 x 10cm (4 x 4in). Roll the paper into tight balls to make holly berries. Make a hole in the side of each berry with a pencil.

11 Dab a little PVA glue in each hole then stick the berries to the ends of the branches. Cut a 4cm (1½in) wide strip of red tissue paper to fit around the plant pot. Fringe it and then wrap it around the top of the pot and tape it in place.

12 To make the angel, trace the pattern on page 112 and transfer it onto thin white card to make a template. Use the template to cut a pair of wings from gold paper and a dress from patterned paper. Cut hair from silver paper and punch two dots from pink paper to make cheeks. Glue a small section of silver doily to the back of the angel's head as a halo. Glue everything in place.

13 Draw on the angel's face with a thin black pen. Gently curve round the angel's dress to make a cone shape and glue the sides together. Place the angel at the top of the tree.

14 To make the star decorations, trace the star pattern from page 112 and transfer it 11 times to thin white card. Cut out the stars. Cut 11 lengths of thin gold wire 10cm (4in) long and fold them in half.

15 Tape the wires to the stars to make hangers. Glue the stars onto gold or silver paper and then cut them out. Hang the star decorations from the branches as the finishing touch.

Templates

Here are the templates you need to complete the projects in this book. They are either full size or half size. Enlarge them if required as indicated beside each template or adjust their size to your own requirements. Instructions on using templates are provided on page 8.

Pop-up Butterfly Card - Page 9

Heart Frame - Page 10

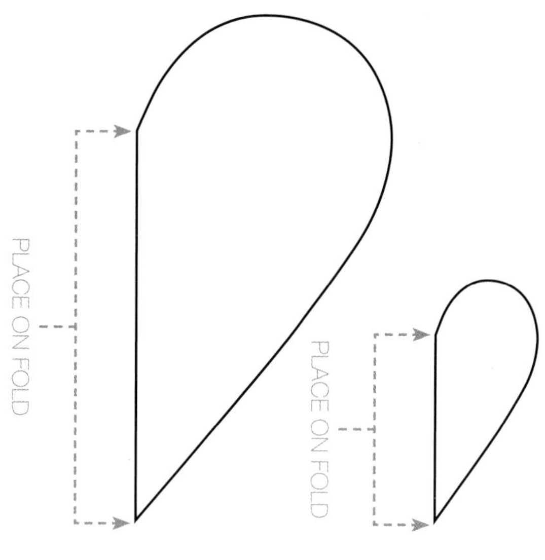

Lacy Flower Card - Page 41

Loving Album Card - Page 25

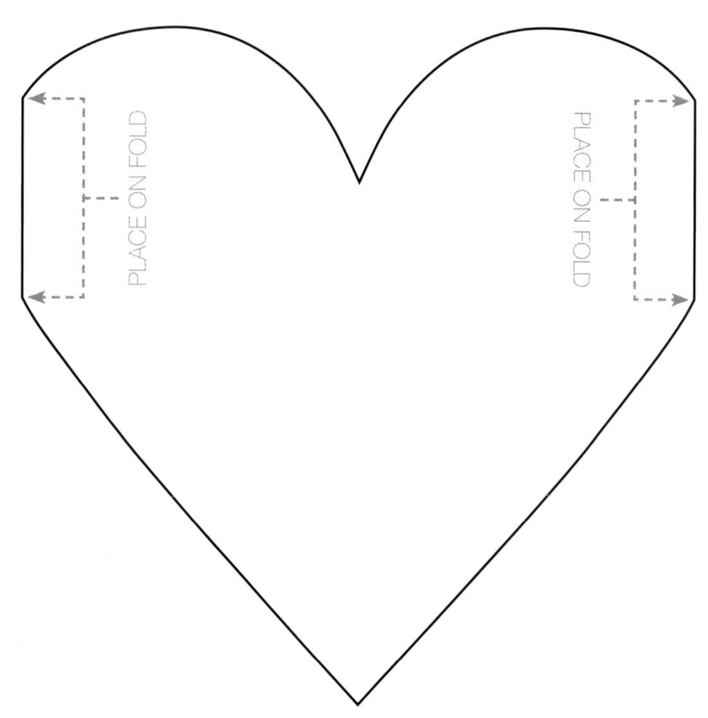

Christmas Hanging Stars - Page 14

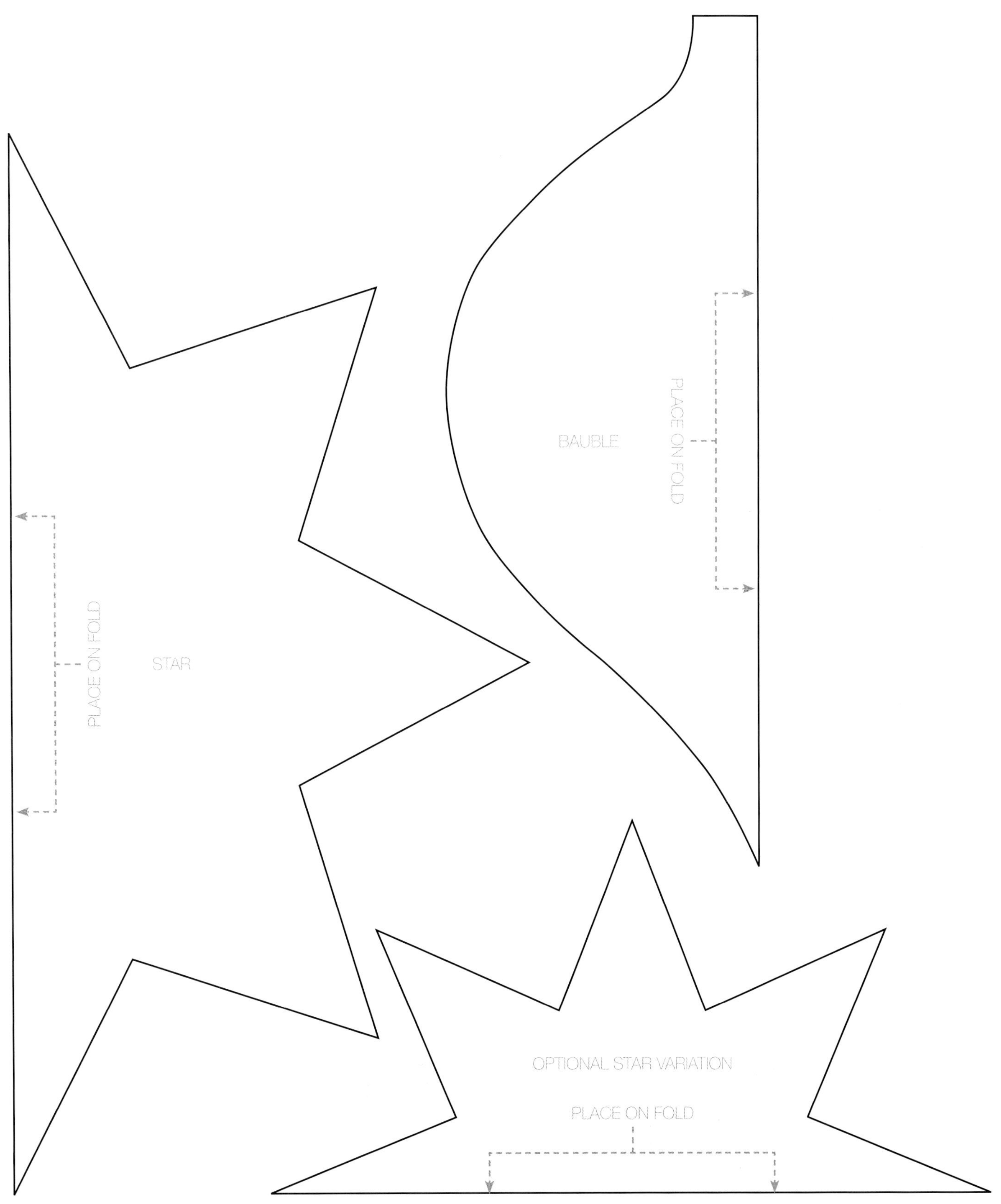

Family-tree Album Cover - Page 18

enlarge by 200%

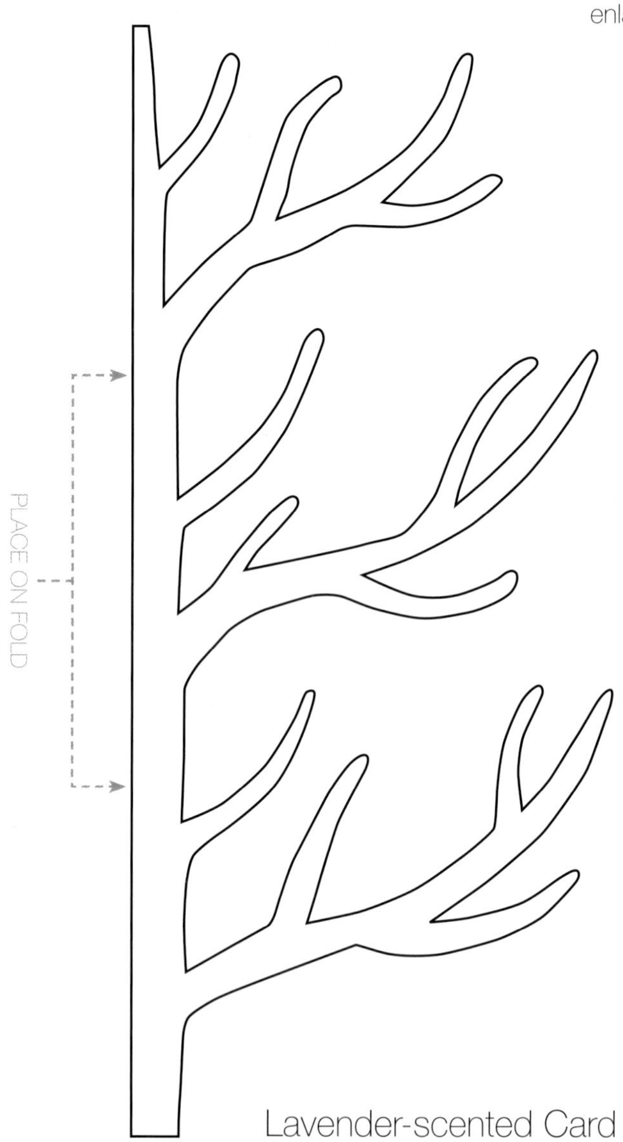

PLACE ON FOLD

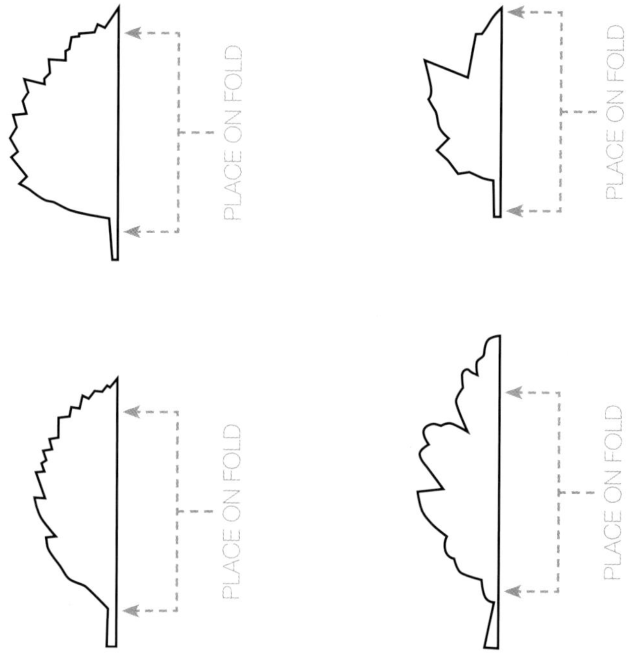

PLACE ON FOLD

PLACE ON FOLD

PLACE ON FOLD

PLACE ON FOLD

Lavender-scented Card - Page 73

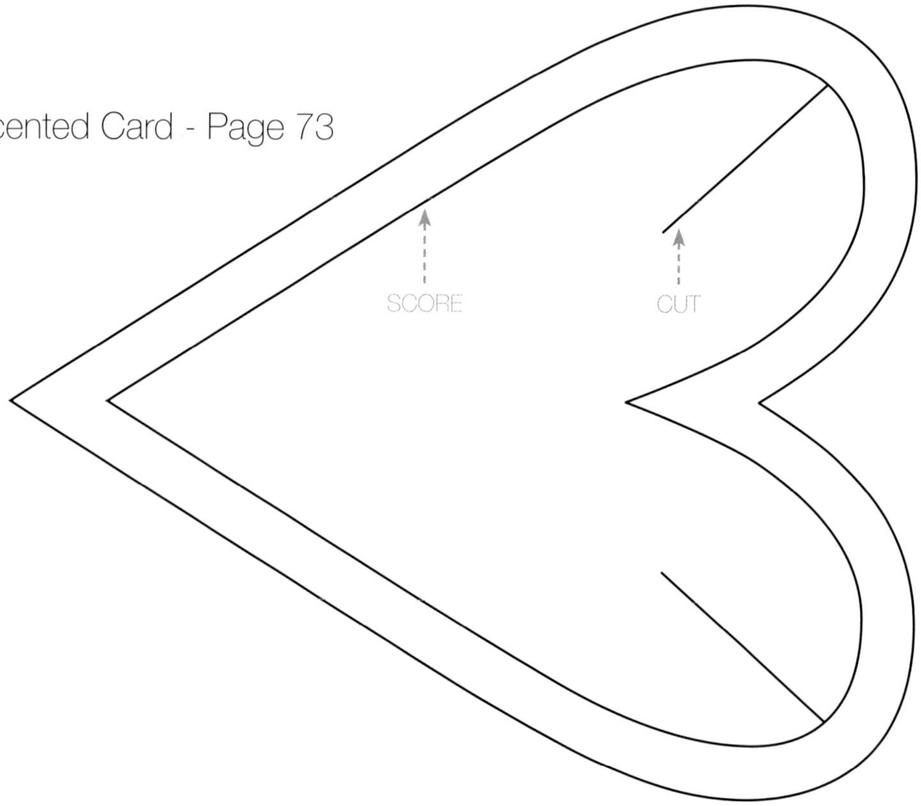

SCORE

CUT

Wedding Garland - Page 26

New Baby Garland - Page 30

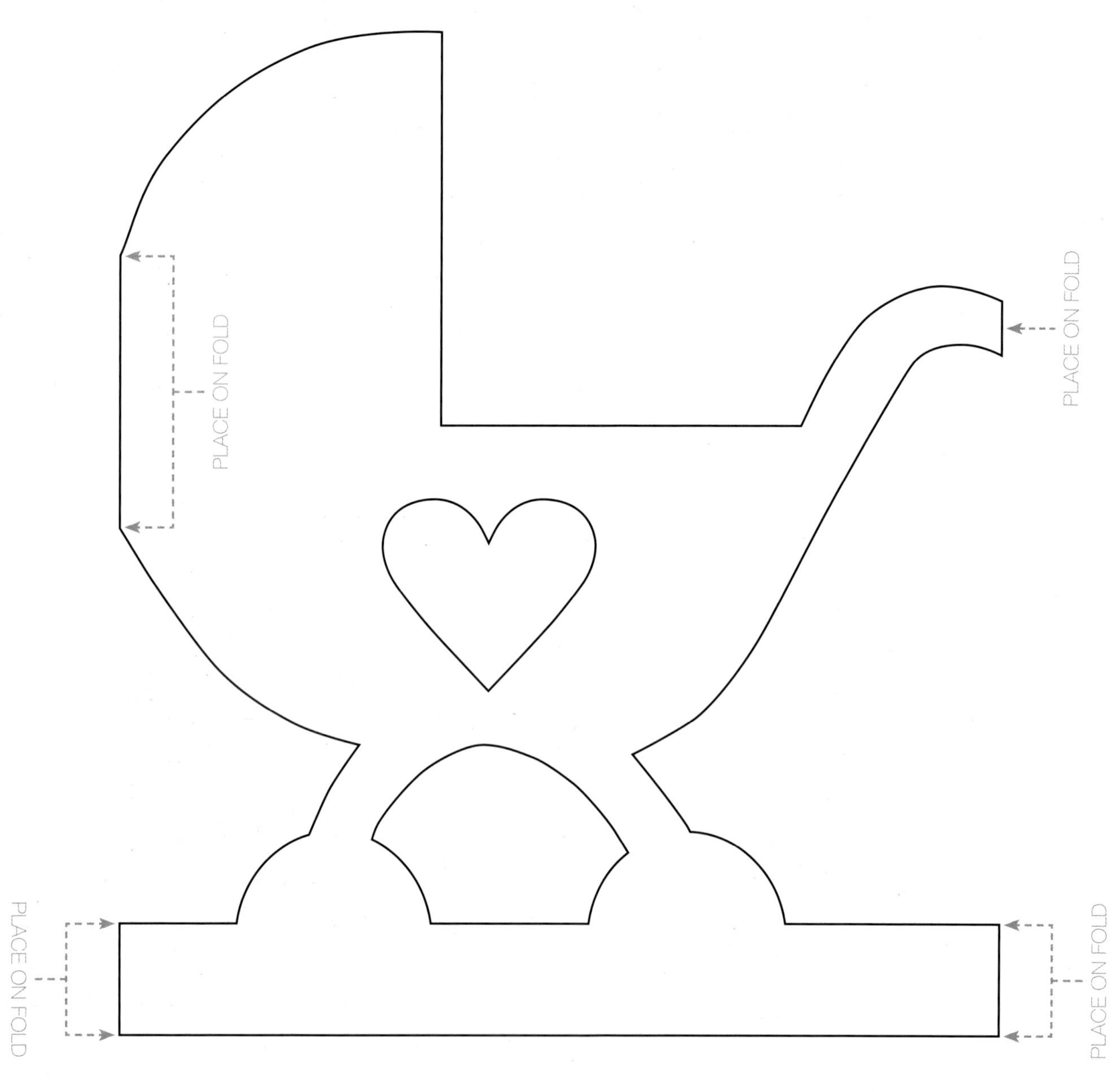

Pirate Pennants - Page 34

Enlarge by 200%

Snowflake Tea Lights - Page 42

Card of Peace - Page 57

Halloween Window - Page 52

Enlarge by 200%

PLACE ON FOLD

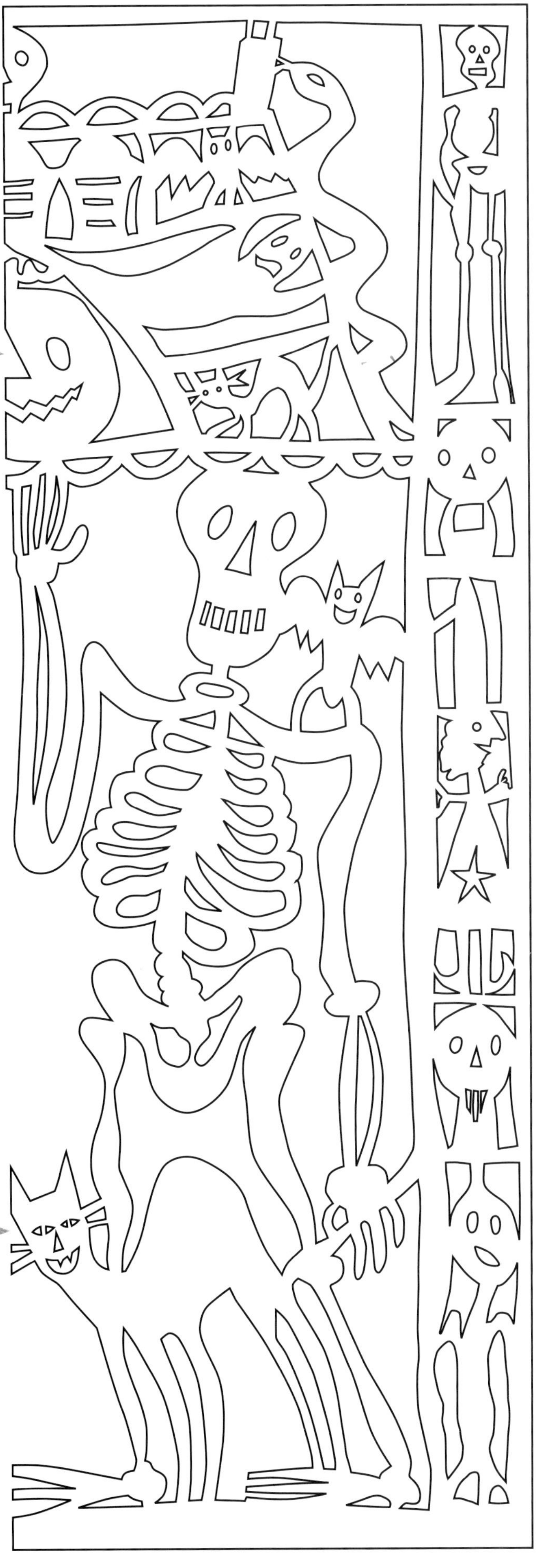

PLACE ON FOLD

Chinese Chandelier - Page 46

Enlarge by 200%

PLACE ON FOLD

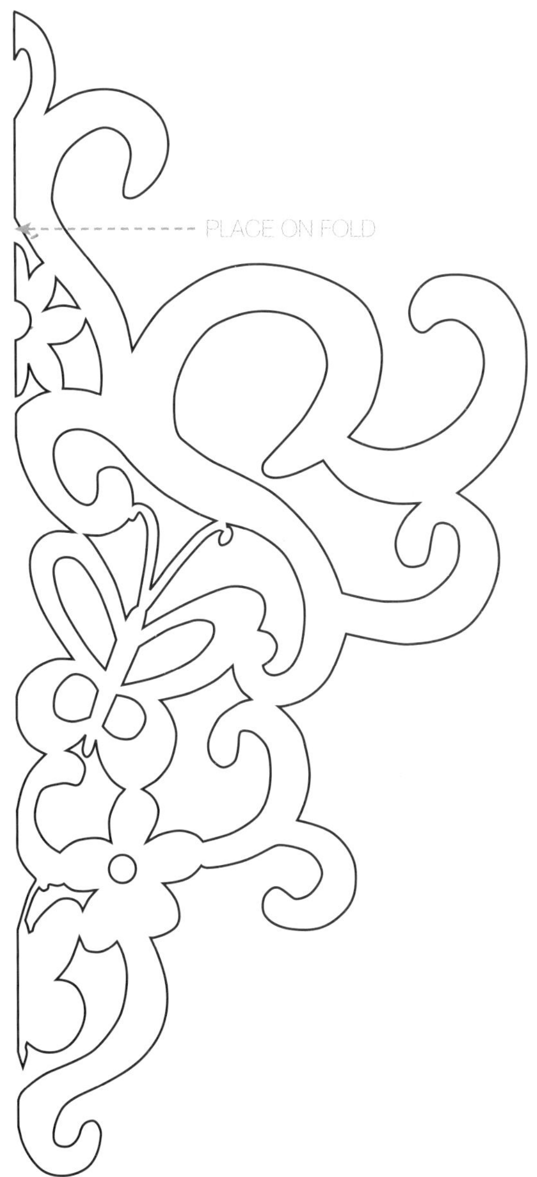

Nursery Carousel Mobile - Page 58

Enlarge by 200%

CONTINUE TRACING
FIRST HORSE AGAIN

Mini Christmas Tree - Page 98

Fairy Jewellery Box - Page 68

Christmas Table Runner - Page 62

Enlarge by 200%

Christmas Table Runner - Page 62

Enlarge by 200%

Easter Chicken Basket - Page 78

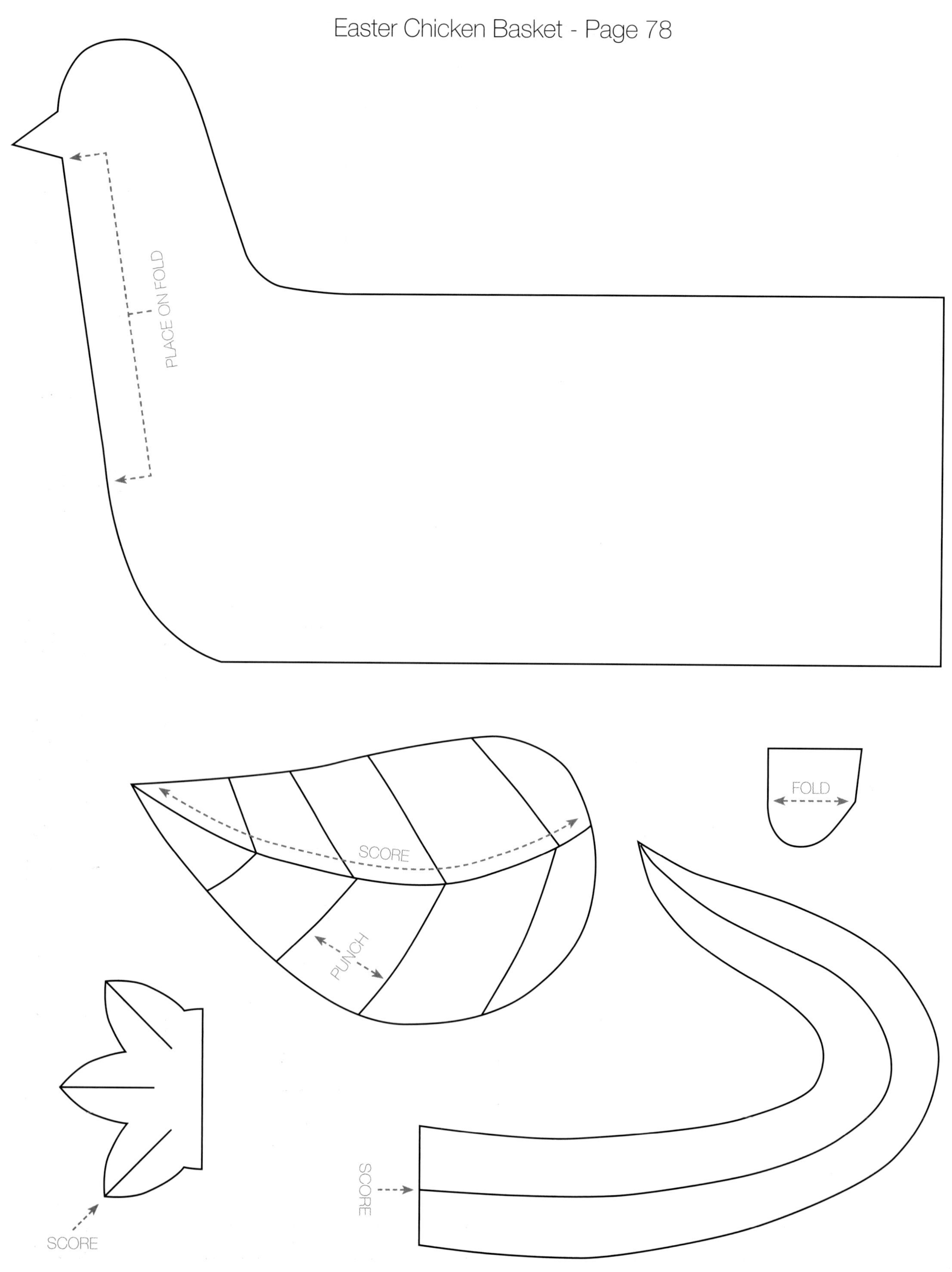

Gingerbread House - Page 82

Enlarge by 200%

Lion Card - Page 89

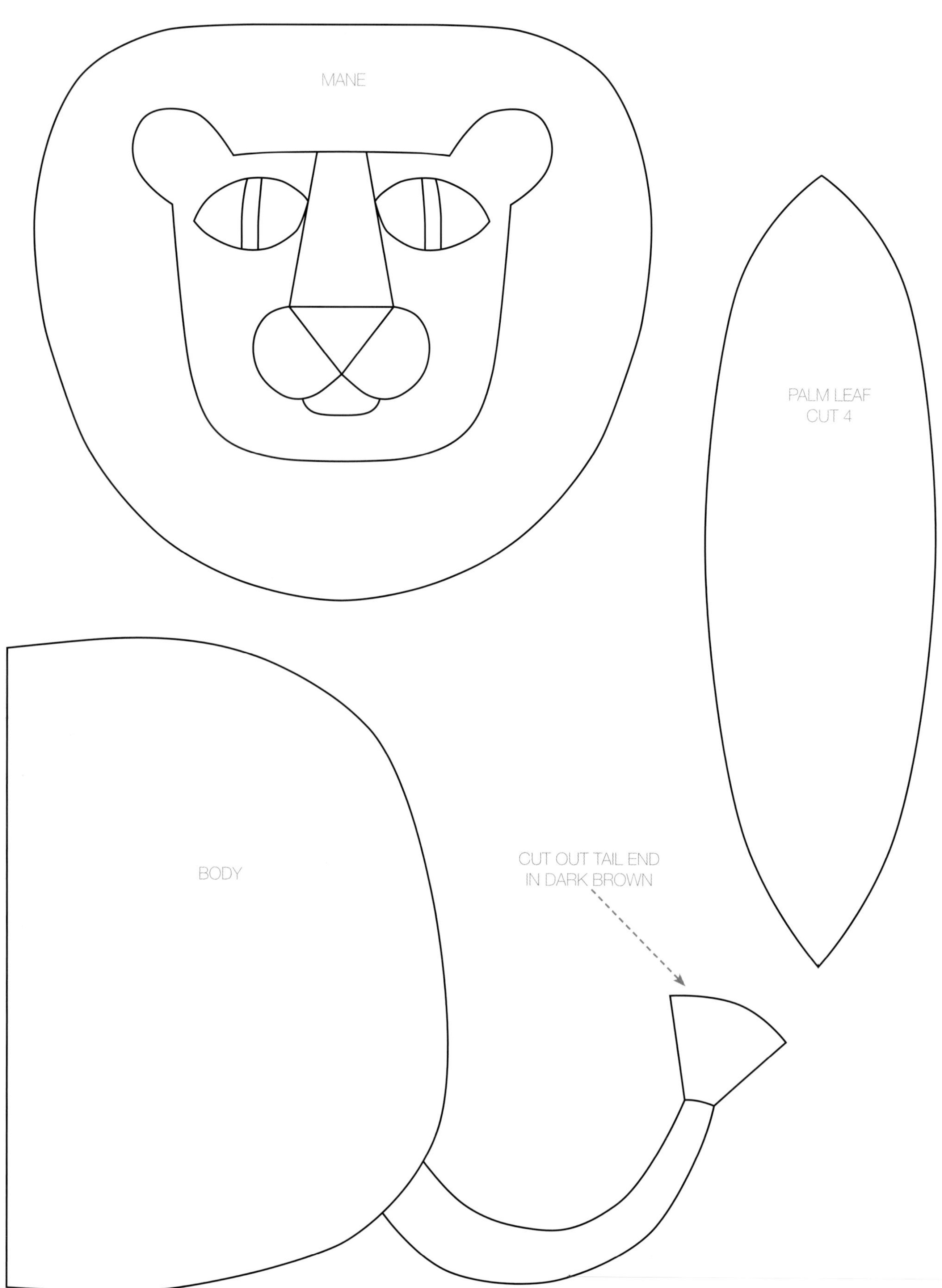

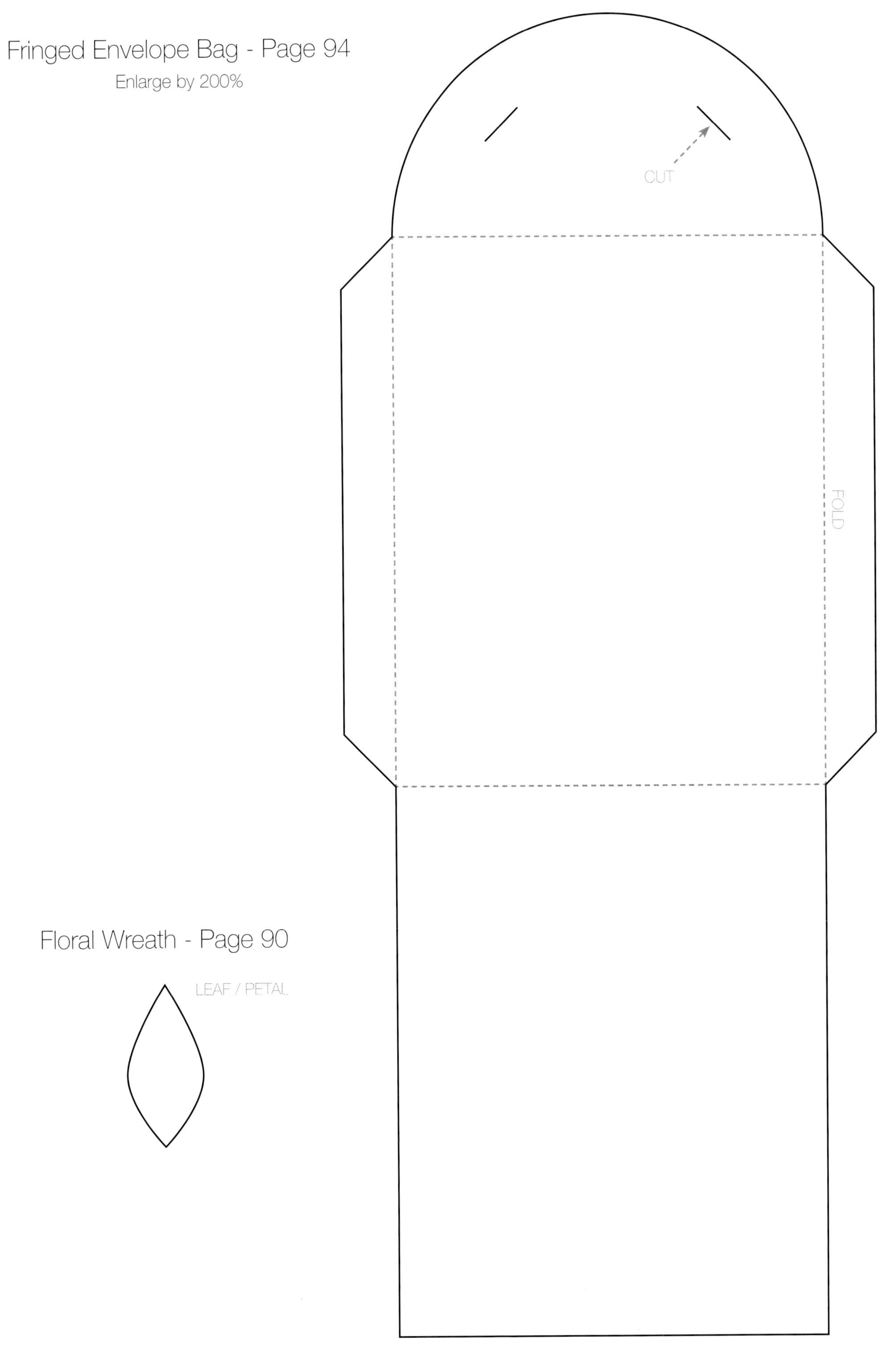
Fringed Envelope Bag - Page 94
Enlarge by 200%
CUT
FOLD
Floral Wreath - Page 90
LEAF / PETAL

Suppliers

UK Suppliers

Book Ends
25–28 Thurloe Place
South Kensington
London SW7 2HQ
Tel: 020 7589 2285
email: bookend@beconnect.com
Specialists in paper crafts, origami paper and many other craft products.

e-crafts.co.uk
Tel: 01384 236000
Wide range of decorative papers.

Fred Aldous
37 Lever Street
Manchester M1 1LW
www.fredaldous.co.uk
Mail order tel: 08707 517 301
Wide range of craft equipment including good selection of shaped scissors.

Hobbycraft
Hobbycraft.co.uk
Wide range of craft equipment and papers.

Lawrence Art Supplies
Shops in Hove and Redruth,
Cornwall
Mail order: www.lawrence.co.uk
Tel: 0845 644 3232
Artists' materials and a good range of papers, including many handmade Japanese varieties.

Paperchase
213–215 Tottenham Court Road
London W1T 7PS
For mail order and details of other branches throughout UK
Tel: 0207 467 6200
Extensive range of decorative and plain papers.

The Paper Warehouse
Grosvenor House Papers Ltd
Westmorland Business Park
Kendal LA9 6NP
Tel: 01539 726161
email: info@ghpkendal.co.uk
www.ghpkendal.co.uk
General craft retailer of a wide range of paper craft supplies including punches and peel-offs.

Squires Model and Craft Tools
100 London Road
Bognor Regis
West Sussex PO21 1DD
Mail order tel: 01243 842424
Exhaustive range of art and craft papers, also model makers' tools including traditional and rotating knives and traditional/decorative edge scissors.

US Suppliers

Fascinating Folds
PO Box 10070
Glendale AZ 85318
www.fascinating-folds.com
An extensive supplier of reference materials for paper craft.

Hollanders Decorative and Handmade Papers
410 N Fourth Avenue
Ann Arbor NI 48104
Tel: 734 741 7531
www.hollanders.com
Supplier of unique decorative papers plus stationery.

Paperarts
www.paperarts.com (Arizona)
Wide range of exciting papers.

Papermojo
papermojo.com
Tel: 1 800 420 3818

Twinrocker Handmade Paper
100 East 3rd Street
Brookston
IN 47923
www.twinrocker.com
Supplier of handmade paper and importer of decorative papers.

Acknowledgments

I would like to thank everyone who has been involved in the production of this book, it has been a pleasure to work with you all. Special thanks to Cheryl Brown for overseeing the whole project from beginning to end, with good humour, enthusiasm and invaluable insights. Also to Karl Adamson for his perfect step photography, and for taking such care, as usual. Thanks to Bethany Dymond, unflappable editor, for her patience and for blending it all together seamlessly, Pru Rodgers for her immaculate art direction, and Betsy Hosegood for casting her eagle eye over the proceedings. Thanks also to Alistair Barnes for his stylish layouts, which reflected the designs so well. Also, thank you Stella, George, Annie and Joe and the Elliots for your pictures. The biggest thank you of all goes to Neil and Stella, who waded through tiny scraps of paper for weeks without complaining, even though dinner was always late.

Index

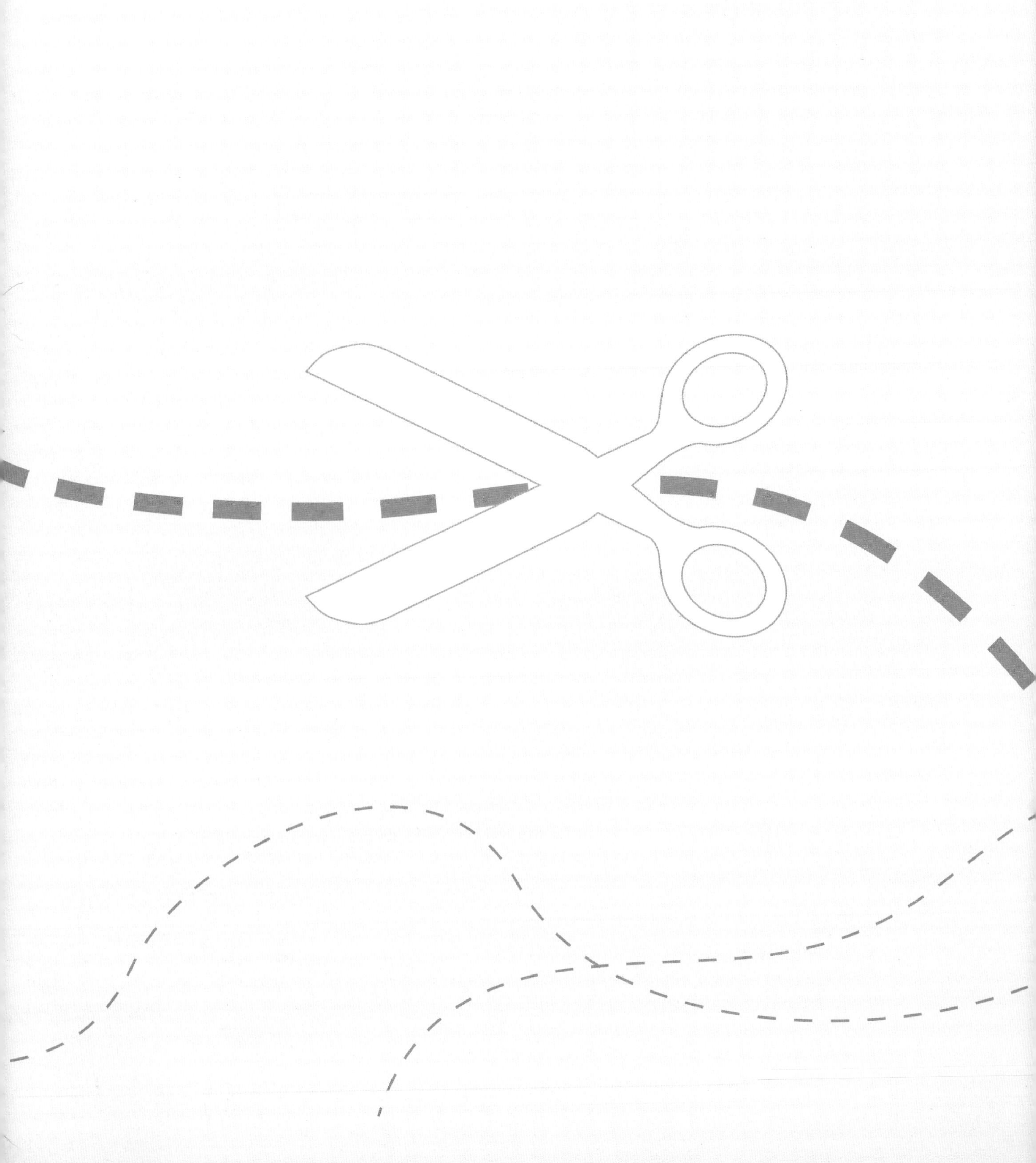